How Shanghai Does It

DIRECTIONS IN DEVELOPMENT
Human Development

How Shanghai Does It

Insights and Lessons from the Highest-Ranking Education System in the World

Xiaoyan Liang, Huma Kidwai, and Minxuan Zhang

WORLD BANK GROUP

Contents

Figures

Tables

Foreword

Education is widely recognized as a fundamental right and as one of the most powerful instruments for economic growth and poverty alleviation. Education is critical to the World Bank Group's mission to end extreme poverty and boost shared prosperity in the world by 2030. It also features prominently in the Sustainable Development Goals adopted by the United Nations in 2015 to transform the world. The fourth of these global goals calls for access to quality education and lifelong learning opportunities for all. In fact, quality education is essential for any country aiming for sustained and diversified economic growth.

The question that policy makers are constantly asking is *how* to achieve quality in education in the face of daunting challenges. The World Bank's Education Strategy 2020 calls for investing early, investing smartly, and investing for all—with a particular emphasis on strengthening education systems and raising learning outcomes. Worldwide, education systems differ in history, context, policy focus, and implementation, as well as results. Through its financing, development knowledge, and global partnerships, the World Bank Group aspires to bring the best global and comparative evidence to individual country contexts. This study, *How Shanghai Does It*, provides many exciting, valuable, and relevant lessons from Shanghai, one of the world's best-performing education systems according to the Organisation for Economic Co-operation and Development's (OECD's) Program for International Student Assessment (PISA).

By analyzing and benchmarking education policies and practices pertaining to teachers, school financing, student assessment, and school autonomy and accountability, the study provides an unparalleled and comprehensive account of the insights and lessons from Shanghai. The account reveals that Shanghai has managed to strategically plan, develop, and establish a set of highly coherent and synergistic education policies that have together boosted education results. Furthermore, the study reveals a second secret—that Shanghai implements its education policies consistently and constantly strives to innovate and reform to meet new challenges. The breadth of the information and analysis in this study is both practical and relevant, not only for education systems aspiring to achieve Shanghai's success, but for Shanghai itself in view of the rapidly changing landscape of social demography and educational purpose and technology in the region and globally.

One of the most impressive aspects of Shanghai's education system is its process for development and management of teachers. Teaching is a well-respected profession, not so much because of the level of pay teachers receive, but rather because of the society's respect for the profession, sustained through long-term, rigorous preservice education and pervasive school-based professional development. Both of these attributes are linked to a well-structured professional career ladder and performance evaluation system. Teachers are expected to be active researchers who constantly reflect on their pedagogy and implement innovations in relation to student outcomes. Principals are strong instructional leaders who can provide guidance on teaching and learning and who understand how best to evaluate teachers. Teachers and principals alike maintain a high level of professional accountability.

What Shanghai has to offer the world is not just its past or even its present, but the future it intends to create for the country as a leading economy in the East Asia and Pacific region, and in the world beyond. In a way, Shanghai itself has already moved beyond PISA and is deliberating even harder questions and challenges, such as the social-emotional well-being of its children, global citizenship, and environmental consciousness, creativity, and innovation.

Shanghai's long-term vision and persistent efforts to reflect on and reform long-held educational traditions, values, and practices are a source of inspiration to the international education and development community.

Claudia Maria Costin   Bert Hofman
Senior Director of Education   *China Country Director*
World Bank   *World Bank*

Acknowledgments

This report was prepared by Xiaoyan Liang, Huma Kidwai, and Minxuan Zhang. Shuang Chen and Yinan Zhang provided excellent background research. A highly competent team of researchers from Shanghai Normal University, including Dr. Wenle Yan, Ms. Qingqing Song, Dr. Bo Ning, Mr. Youyuan Wang, Mr. Xiaohu Zhu, Mr. Hui Chen, Ms. Yun Zhou, Ms. Chunhua Zhao, and Ms. Jingjing Liu, made significant contributions to the report. They painstakingly collected policy data for the Systems Approach for Better Education Results (SABER) modules, answered many rounds of questions, and further facilitated school visits and interviews in Shanghai for the World Bank team.

Within the Bank, the team is grateful to the technical assistance provided by the various SABER teams, including Halsey Rogers and Andrew Paul Trembley for SABER–Teacher and SABER–School Finance, Angela Demas for SABER–School Autonomy and Accountability, and Margarite Clarke for SABER–Student Assessment.

Valuable comments were received from peer reviewers, including Hana Brixi (Program Leader), Barbara Bruns (Lead Education Specialist, World Bank), Juan Manuel Moreno (Lead Education Specialist and the World Bank's Global Lead for Basic Education), and Dandan Chen (Practice Leader). The team further owes gratitude to the extremely supportive World Bank senior management, including China Country Director Bert Hofman, Senior Director for Education Claudia Maria Costin, Director of Education Amit Dar, and Education Manager for East Asia and Pacific (EAP) Harry Anthony Patrinos, who was the first to encourage the team and provided initial financing for the study before he became the EAP Education Manager. The work would not have happened without the strong endorsement and support from Luis Benveniste, who was the previous Education Manager for EAP, and China Human Development Program Leader Elena Glinskaya.

About the Authors

Dr. Xiaoyan Liang is a Senior Education Specialist and the World Bank's Education Team Leader for China, Malaysia, Mongolia, and the Republic of Korea. Dr. Liang joined the World Bank as a Young Professional almost two decades ago, after graduating from Harvard University with a doctor of education degree. Since then, she has led policy analysis and dialogue and managed education programs in African, Latin American, and East Asian countries. Dr. Liang is passionate about development through education and has solid education policy and program expertise in wide-ranging areas, including early childhood education, technical and vocational education and skills development, higher education and science and technology, education finance, and teacher education. She is widely published on various education topics within and outside the World Bank.

Dr. Huma Kidwai is an education consultant in the World Bank's Education Global Practice, East Asia and Pacific Region. She has a doctorate of education from Columbia University and has conducted extensive research on education reform and faith-based educational institutions in India. Previously, Dr. Kidwai has worked with the Poverty Reduction Group of the World Bank, the Know Violence in Childhood global initiative, the Praxis Institute for Participatory Practices, and the Earth Institute's Columbia Global Centers. Her professional experience includes projects on education, child protection, health, and poverty reduction, with a particular focus on issues of exclusion.

Professor Minxuan Zhang is currently the Director of the Research Institute for International and Comparative Education at Shanghai Normal University and a Fellow of the Consultant Council of the International Institute of Educational Planning, UNESCO. Professor Zhang has had a long and distinguished career and held important positions in education in Shanghai, such as President of Shanghai Normal University, Director of Shanghai PISA, Director of the Shanghai Academy of Educational Sciences, Deputy Education Commissioner in Shanghai, and Principal of the Shanghai Experimental School. Professor Zhang is a globally recognized education expert and remains active in advising various ministries of education on education policies.

Executive Summary

This report, *How Shanghai Does It: Insights and Lessons from the Highest-Ranking Education System in the World*, presents an in-depth examination of how students in Shanghai achieved the highest scores in the areas of reading, science, and mathematics on a respected global assessment of 15-year-olds' educational abilities. It documents and benchmarks key policies in Shanghai's basic education, provides evidence on the extent to which these policies have been implemented in schools, and explores how these policies and their implementation have affected learning outcomes.

The report uses the World Bank's Systems Approach for Better Education Results (SABER) as an organizing framework to organize and benchmark policies. School-based surveys and other existing research are employed to shed light on educational impact and implementation. Programme for International Student Assessment (PISA) 2012 data are used to analyze the variations in Shanghai students' achievement and to examine the extent to which school variables may be associated with variation after accounting for family and student background.

Based on the SABER framework and rubric, Shanghai scored "established" and "advanced" in almost all areas across four key educational domains: teachers, school finance, school autonomy and accountability, and student assessment. SABER rated school accountability and role of the school council in governance as "emerging" (appendix A).

One finding is that Shanghai has a high degree of coherence between policy and implementation. The study does not find significant divergence between policy statements and reality. This noteworthy connection between policy and implementation can possibly be attributed to a number of factors, including the cultural and historical Chinese characteristics of top-down and centralized government administration; close monitoring of the programs and policies and alignment of performance with incentives; high levels of professional accountability among teachers, principals, and administrators within the education system; and, to some extent, modest and realistic policy statements and goals.

Shanghai also stands out for its constant drive to renew and improve its education system and practices. The city has been on a journey of educational reform ever since China opened up to the world in the 1800s, when western missionaries established new western-style schools. Reform efforts have further intensified during the past three decades, subsequent to the Cultural Revolution in the 1970s. Three key strategic documents issued by the Chinese State Council during this period have guided national education reform in three distinct phases. The documents include "Decisions about Education System Reform" (1988), "Decisions on Deepening Education Reform and Promoting Quality-Oriented Education in an All-Round Way" (1999), and "China's Medium- and Long-Term Education Reform and Development Plan Outline" (2010). The city has been a pioneer and leader of the national education reform movement and is now making plans for new reforms through 2050. The following sections summarize key policy highlights and describe some main policy considerations as Shanghai continues along its educational reform path.

Attracting and Developing an Excellent Teaching Force

Clear learning objectives and standards, compact and well-aligned teaching learning materials, and efficient evaluation systems for all subjects across all grade levels provide the framework for teachers in Shanghai. The Teachers Law of the People's Republic of China (1993) defines teachers' general obligations and working hours. Not only should teachers fulfill teaching contracts and carry out the school teaching plan, but they should also dedicate themselves to the moral, physical, and intellectual development of students and organize relevant student learning activities. The Teachers Law also requires teachers to improve their own moral ethics and pedagogical expertise. Teacher responsibilities go beyond the classroom to encompass professional development and extracurricular activities.

Teaching in Shanghai is an attractive and respected middle-class profession. The working conditions, such as educational facilities and student-to-teacher ratios, are attractive, and clear career advancement mechanisms are in place. Shanghai requires at least a three-year tertiary education for primary school teachers and a four-year university education for secondary school teachers. In practice, however, the academic requirement is more stringent, and most teachers in Shanghai have at least a bachelor's degree. Teachers fulfill a one-year probationary period before being formally hired by the school districts.

The city offers teachers incentives to teach in hard-to-staff rural and semi-urban schools. It transfers and rotates teachers to help underperforming schools and disadvantaged student populations. Teachers and principals working in hardship areas can advance more quickly in their careers. Although Shanghai does not face a critical teacher shortage in any particular subject, a disparity remains in the allocation of teachers and other resources between rural and central urban districts.

Recruitment criteria for school principals are high and stringently adhered to, with a clear focus on instructional leadership. But detailed qualification requirements vary across districts. Principals in Shanghai participate in various leadership programs, based on the "Professional Standards for Basic Education Principals," over the course of their tenure. Principals have opportunities for career advancement. The city links part of principals' pay to the overall performance of their schools. It also explicitly expects principals to be instructional leaders. Most principals in Shanghai observe between 30 and 50 classes per semester and provide feedback to teachers.

Results from a series of student assessments serve a diagnostic purpose for monitoring and evaluating teachers. Teacher performance is monitored using multiple mechanisms, not just students' academic achievement. These processes include frequent district-level inspections of teachers' work and classroom observations by senior teachers and principals.

Shanghai designs professional development activities to be collaborative and to focus on instructional improvement. School principals are responsible for creating targeted teacher training plans based on each teacher's evaluation results. Professional development is often a substantial part of schools' operational expenditure. The city pairs weak and inexperienced teachers with high-performing and experienced ones. Important platforms for teacher professional development and performance evaluation—teaching-research groups and lesson observations—are also practiced universally in schools. Teachers are expected to be researchers who would evaluate and modify their own pedagogy in relation to student outcomes. The city requires new teachers to complete at least 360 hours of professional development in their first five years of service, and an additional 540 hours to be considered for a senior rank.

The city rewards good teachers. Performance affects promotional opportunities, and a small part of teacher pay reflects workload and performance. Policy guidelines require teachers to be accredited once every five years to continue teaching. The city can dismiss teachers for misconduct, child abuse, or poor performance, but these events are rare. In cases of poor performance, transfers and early retirement are the more commonly observed reprimanding practices.

Overall, Shanghai is characterized by a coherent and comprehensive system of teacher professional development that incorporates multiple layers of in-service training, school-based teacher research groups, evaluation of teacher performance, and a structured career ladder that provides both motivation and a mechanism for teachers to progress in their careers, which is key to Shanghai's demonstrated excellence in education.

Financing Education for Quality and Equity

Detailed policies and regulations are in place to ensure minimum educational inputs of infrastructure, staffing norms, learning materials, and teacher qualifications. The education budget is channeled to schools via teacher salaries, capital investment, and an operational budget based on the number of students. However, because of the decentralized nature of education financing, in which each district finances its own basic education, disparities remain across districts and between city and rural schools. Shanghai's public expenditure on education as a share of GDP was about 3.5 percent in 2013, a smaller proportion than spent by other high-performing economies such as Finland, Japan, the Republic of Korea, and the United States.

The system increasingly designs education financing to ensure that it lifts all students' learning outcomes by assisting low-performing schools and districts through financial and other means. Shanghai has discarded the inequitable basic education "key school" system[1] and is instead focusing on making every neighborhood school excellent. Innovative financing instruments such as "entrusted management," which pairs low-performing schools with high-performing peer institutions, is rapidly gaining support. The municipal government transfers half of education surplus taxes to economically weak districts and mandates that top secondary schools reserve some spaces for middle school graduates from poor districts.

Shanghai closely monitors the school management environment and teaching-learning outcomes. The municipality collects school and district data annually. However, Shanghai could improve the way it uses information and communications technologies to collect data. Efforts are being made in this regard. In 2010, based on the lessons from PISA, the Shanghai Municipal Education Commission established its own quality-monitoring system called "Green Indicators of Academic Quality of Primary and Secondary School Students," also known as Green Indicators. The main objective was to assess school quality holistically, including academic rigor, teaching motivation, and student-teacher relationships. Shanghai has a city-level system for determining the school's annual calendar, and mechanisms are in place to monitor the availability of school learning materials and physical resources.

Education budgeting is based on adequate and transparent information and made available to the public. Data are collected at the school and district level to adequately inform future budget planning. Internal and external audit systems are in place to verify the use of educational resources. Schools that fail internal or external audits receive legal sanctions.

Shanghai has specific policies to assist disadvantaged students with education expenses. The city provides free school meals for migrant children and students living below the poverty line, and provides education subsidies to students with disabilities or economic hardships. Shanghai has made more progress in attaining equitable access to schooling than any other region in China according to the 2015 National Compulsory Education Quality Monitoring Assessment.[2] Migrant children, however, continue to face barriers in accessing local public compulsory education schools. These children cannot always produce the necessary documents to prove their family's working status and they cannot access Shanghai's public senior secondary schools after completing the nine-year basic education. The city should further implement special education and strengthen efforts to help migrant and other disadvantaged children.

Balancing School Autonomy and Accountability

Schools in Shanghai are afforded a high level of autonomy in planning and managing the school budget. Budget planning is a collaborative and multistep process. After receiving budget approval from the district Department of Finance and the municipal government, schools can execute the budget under defined categories. Schools have limited influence over teachers' base pay scale, which is set at the municipal level, but have the autonomy to allocate merit-based pay. The school wage bill is divided into two parts: The base salary of teachers makes up 70 percent of the total wage budget. The remaining 30 percent is distributed on the basis of work load and performance. Schools tend to have more say in determining the salaries of nonteaching staff. Public schools have less autonomy than private schools, particularly in their ability to raise funds. Detailed guidelines are in place for regulating financial management and transparency standards in public and private schools. Compliance failure leads to legal sanctions.

Schools have substantial autonomy in personnel management. Based on their district, schools have varying levels of autonomy to appoint and dismiss teachers. Schools in principle have the authority to hire and fire teachers, but in practice they can only hire additional teachers if their quota is raised. Otherwise they can only hire teachers on short-term contracts. Teachers are rarely fired. The hiring and deployment process for nonteaching staff is more flexible. Mechanisms are in place for schools to participate in teacher recruitment and select the preferred candidates.

Private school principals in Shanghai tend to exercise greater autonomy over staff and pay-related decisions than do public school principals. Shanghai does not have a uniform municipal-level policy on the appointment and deployment of principals; districts have the authority to establish their own processes. Districts usually maintain and cultivate a pool of principal candidates over a sustained period before formal recruitment.

In addition to complying with financial management guidelines, schools are also accountable for school management and learning outcomes. The city inspects schools annually and comprehensively evaluates them with the Green Indicators. It uses a well-established and frequently administered system of school assessments to inform teaching practices and make necessary adjustments and also conducts citywide examinations annually at the end of ninth and twelfth grades. China's first nationwide basic-education quality assessment was conducted in 2015. Shanghai is also the first Chinese province or city to have participated in the international PISA since 2009. The rich set of student data helps policy makers track student learning outcome trends. One positive observation is that Shanghai has made an effort not to rank or publish individual student exam results or to use exam results as an explicit mechanism for teacher rewards or sanctions.

Shanghai schools have some autonomy in curriculum and pedagogy. At the central level, the Ministry of Education sets overall national curriculum standards for all subjects. Shanghai, along with a few selected provinces, is allowed to have its own curriculum and has released its subject-specific "Curriculum Plan for Regular Elementary and Secondary Schools in Shanghai." Shanghai schools further have the autonomy to design 30 percent of the curriculum as school-based curriculum, according to each school's strengths and the areas of their curricular focus. Furthermore, teachers have a certain level of pedagogical autonomy.

The system promotes and maintains professional accountability through relations within the teaching staff and through the execution of in-service teacher training and monitoring procedures. As school principals and senior teachers engage with others through teaching-research groups and through other support and mentoring methods, professional accountability becomes more apparent.

Public schools are not mandated to have school councils but follow the "school principal responsibility system," in which principals make key decisions, usually in consultation with party secretaries and increasingly in consultation with teacher staff associations. Private schools in Shanghai are legally required to establish "school boards." Although the boards participate in decision making on general planning and budgeting, they are generally not involved in professional teaching and learning matters. Parent-teacher associations, formed beginning in 2012, are limited to supporting basic school management tasks and helping students learn at home. There is no city guideline, manual, or policy regulating the participation of the community in school activities and learning inputs.

No explicit policies or public forums are in place for expressing accountability to stakeholders. Communities and parents trust educational professionals to manage their professional affairs and to educate.

Creating an Effective Student Assessment System

The common formats for student assessment used in China and Shanghai are those of continuous and formative classroom assessments, summative examinations particularly at the end of ninth grade (*zhong kao*) and twelfth grade (*gao kao*), and national and international large-scale assessments. Classroom assessments are frequent and are executed in a variety of formats, such as quizzes, oral tests, presentations, home assignments, and so forth, allowing students greater possibilities for demonstrating their learning based on their abilities than afforded by summative examinations that mostly tend to be written tests.

There are clear guidelines on assessment standards, and efforts have been made to align these standards with appropriate, age-relevant expected learning outcomes. It has been ascertained that efforts are made to monitor the quality of assessments at the school level, and the data are effectively used to inform teaching-learning and future assessment practices in the classroom. As part of government efforts to improve education quality the State Council formally rolled out the Plan for National Compulsory Education Quality Monitoring in April 2015. In 2011, the Shanghai Municipal Educational Commission also launched a series of surveys entitled "Green Indicators of Academic Quality of Primary and Secondary School Students." The surveys aim to improve educational management and the educational ecology. The indicators include student academic achievement, student learning motivation, student academic workload, teacher-student relations, teachers' instruction styles, and the annual progress on such indicators. The surveys are aimed at all primary and junior secondary students in the compulsory education stage. To further improve classroom assessment, the municipal and district-level Teaching Research Offices undertake regular research projects on the status of student assessments to inform policy decisions.

Senior secondary entrance and graduation exams are well-recognized social events in Shanghai and are closely followed by students, parents, educators, and the media. Effective execution of these exams is enabled by a well-structured system with clear policy guidelines, regular funding, and sufficient and well-trained human resources. These exams are aligned with learning goals for students and teachers. These exams are considered high in quality and transparent and fair in process. However, the exams are often blamed for creating high pressure on students and motivating schools and teachers to teach to the test. Exam test scores almost exclusively determine whether a student can attend a university and which tier.[3] To alleviate the fear parents and students have of these examinations, the Shanghai Municipal Education Commission is currently making an effort to revise the *gao kao* and *zhong kao* exams to make them more flexible. The new formats will be rolled out in 2017–18.

Shanghai is one of the pioneer Chinese provinces to participate in international large-scale assessments. It performed outstandingly on the 2009 and 2012 PISA and garnered significant national and international attention for its educational success. The enabling context for its participation in PISA, which includes the presences of clear policy guidelines, necessary funding, and effective human resources, were assessed at the "advanced" level. However, it scored rather poorly on its policy goal of ensuring effective use of the data generated through such international assessments.

Linking Policies and Implementation to Learning Outcomes

The extent to which Shanghai's education policies and practices foster learning outcomes is revealed in the 2012 PISA results. Variations are substantial across educational programs, with upper secondary students performing better than lower secondary, and model or experimental senior secondary students performing better than those from vocational schools. Overall, model or experimental upper secondary school students scored the highest across math, science, and reading. Shanghai also emerged as one of the most equitable education systems among the PISA participants, with the highest proportion of disadvantaged students performing among the top 25 percent of students after controlling for socioeconomic status.

The between-program variation in PISA scores is greater than the within-program variation, indicating that the system efficiently places students into different programs at the end of lower secondary school based on test scores. However, the analysis performed for this report was able to show that within each of the program types, policies and practices at the school level play a significant role in explaining students' PISA performance. School factors that are positively associated with PISA performance largely fall into the following categories: educational resources, extracurricular activities, principal instructional leadership, curriculum autonomy (slightly negative on math performance in lower secondary school), accountability (vocational schools with more parental pressure do better in math), and teacher participation in school governance (positive on math at the upper secondary level).

Moreover, individual and family background characteristics have demonstrated consistent correlation with student performance across academic programs. Girls perform significantly worse on math and science and better on reading than boys, consistent with findings from other PISA participants.[4] Home educational resources, cultural possessions, and parental education are positively associated with student literacy. In contrast, family wealth is negatively related to performance. Students who have attended at least a year of preschool perform significantly better on all three domains.

Policy Considerations for Shanghai

The comprehensive assessment and benchmarking of education policies provides an opportunity to reflect on a few considerations for Shanghai.

Consider delaying tracking to tenth grade or later. The *zhong kao* exam after ninth grade tracks students into three distinct senior secondary programs with very little horizontal mobility between programs. Cumulative differences in endowment in teachers and other resources further accentuate the disparity in education quality among programs. Shanghai could potentially pilot eliminating the *zhong kao* and delaying tracking to tenth or twelfth grades like other advanced nations and provide more curriculum diversification.

Increase assistance to migrant and other disadvantaged children. Shanghai has proactively enacted policies and approaches to expand education services to migrant and other disadvantaged children. However, the current eligibility criteria of three years of residency and employment may need to be relaxed to allow more migrant children to enroll in local public or government-sponsored private schools. "Disadvantaged" children are required to update their status every year to qualify for assistance, which could ostracize them further. The city does not allow migrant children to enroll in its public senior secondary schools, limiting their potential.

Expand the role of parents, the community, and society in education. Parent-teacher associations are a fairly new practice and tend to have limited responsibilities. At the same time, many anecdotes and isolated studies seem to indicate some dissatisfaction with the public education system. Shanghai could consider expanding the role of parents, the community, and society in general in the education system.

Further explore the role of public-private partnerships to address the last-mile issues in education service delivery. Promising initiatives such as entrusted management of low-performing schools and purchase of education services from private providers could be scaled up and formally institutionalized.

Find a healthier balance between academic excellence and students' social and emotional well-being. Though not explicitly discussed in this report, students in Shanghai report more unhappiness and parental pressure compared with their international peers. The city could further encourage institutions to engage in evidence-based education research and public education debates. It could also continue to build a virtuous cycle of reform and development toward an education system that is even more competitive globally.

Notes

1. "Key schools" were schools selected for their records of educational accomplishment and were given priority in assignment of teachers, equipment, and funds. In practice, key schools favored urban areas and were allowed to admit and train high-achieving students for entrance into top universities. The practice was gradually abolished beginning in the late 1980s in stages across different regions of the country.

2. China implemented its first national compulsory education quality assessment in 2015. The sample included about 200,000 fourth- and eighth-grade students in 6,474 primary and middle schools in 323 counties or districts from the 31 Chinese provinces as well as autonomous regions. Students were tested in the two subjects of mathematics and physical education/health. More than 100,000 teachers responded to teacher surveys.

3. Chinese universities are grouped into four tiers: first-tier universities consist of the best Chinese universities; second-tier universities are regular tertiary degree universities; third-tier universities are mainly provincial or city-level universities; and the fourth tier are mainly tertiary technical and vocational education and training colleges. The Ministry of Education announces cutoff scores for each tier after the exam.

4. On the 2009 PISA, boys outperformed girls in mathematics in 35 of the 65 participating countries and economies. In 5 countries, girls outperformed boys, and in 25 countries there was no significant difference between the genders. (Organisation for Economic Co-operation and Development [OECD]. 2011. *PISA 2009 at a Glance*. Paris: OECD Publishing, Paris. http://dx.doi.org/10.1787/9789264095298-en.)

Abbreviations

EMIS	education management information system
GDP	gross domestic product
ICT	information and communications technology
ISCED	International Standard Classification of Education
OECD	Organisation for Economic Co-operation and Development
PISA	Programme for International Student Assessment
PRC	People's Republic of China
PTA	parent-teacher association
SAA	School Autonomy and Accountability
SABER	Systems Approach for Better Education Results (World Bank)
SAR	Special Administrative Region
SHPISA	Shanghai PISA Committee
TALIS	Teaching and Learning International Survey

RMB	renminbi (China's official currency)
US$	U.S. dollars

Introduction

Background

The release of the 2012 Organisation for Economic Co-operation and Development (OECD) Programme for International Student Assessment (PISA) results has sparked another round of discussion and comparison of student achievement across the globe. PISA is an international assessment that measures the capabilities of 15-year-olds in reading, science, and mathematical literacy. In addition, PISA surveys participating students, parents, and school principals on a wide range of detailed and internationally comparable measures of background information, covering students' family characteristics and institutional features of the school systems. PISA has been conducted once every three years since 2000. Specifically, PISA 2012 tested mathematics literacy in depth and updated the assessment of student performance in reading and science in 65 economies. The 2012 PISA also included modules on problem-solving skills and financial literacy.

Among the 65 participating economies in 2012, Shanghai, China, ranked first in mathematics literacy, with a mean score of 613 points, which is 119 points higher than the OECD average (equivalent to approximately three years of schooling). Hong Kong SAR, China; Japan; the Republic of Korea; Liechtenstein; Macao SAR, China; the Netherlands; Singapore; Switzerland; and Taiwan, China, were among the top 10 performers in mathematics. Shanghai also achieved the highest scores in reading and science. Shanghai first participated in the PISA tests in 2009 when it also ranked highest in the three subjects.

An intense discussion has been trailing the Shanghai PISA story since 2009, ranging from initial questioning of the true representativeness of the sample, to attempting to discredit Shanghai's results by saying that Shanghai is not China, or attributing Shanghai and East Asian achievements to merely "Confucius," culture, or parental emphasis on education. In parallel, professional efforts have also tried to "demystify" Shanghai's secrets. Most prominently, Tom Friedman shared his observations on Shanghai's elementary schools in his article "The Shanghai Secret" in the opinions pages of the New York Times on October 22, 2013:

> When you sit in on a class here and meet with the principal and teachers, what you find is a relentless focus on all the basics that we know make for high-performing schools but that are difficult to pull off consistently across an entire school system. These are: a deep commitment to teacher training, peer-to-peer learning and constant professional development, a deep involvement of parents in their children's learning, an insistence by the school's leadership on the highest standards and a culture that prizes education and respects teachers.

In a similar but more global fashion, the OECD put together a series of country education highlights focusing on high-performing countries in a short video program "Strong Performers and Successful Reformers" in 2012. In the video, Shanghai's success was largely attributed to government leadership and a policy focus on improving low-performing schools.

Missing from the picture, however, is a more comprehensive, systematic, in-depth, and objective rendition of the policies and practices of basic education in Shanghai, benchmarked against others in key dimensions. This report, therefore, is an attempt to systematically organize and document the policy and implementation efforts in the realm of basic education in Shanghai. The report uses an existing systems diagnostic and benchmarking tool developed by the World Bank, the Systems Approach for Better Education Results, or SABER, along with supplemental data from school-level principal surveys, existing studies carried out mostly in Chinese, and additional data and information on education expenditures and labor force surveys.

The report also provides extensive analysis of student performance on the 2012 PISA and makes an effort to identify school-level variables that are correlated with variation in student performance across Shanghai. The report attempts to adopt a systems approach, but particular emphasis is placed on teachers, education financing, balancing autonomy and accountability, and student assessment.

The report has three broad audiences in mind. The most relevant audience would be education policy makers from other countries and the rest of China interested in learning more about Shanghai's education system and policies. A second audience would be the relevant education authorities in Shanghai and China, given that the report attempts to benchmark Shanghai against other systems and in the process identify highlights, challenges, and recommendations for future reform in light of other countries' experiences. Finally, because of its scope and depth, the report can serve as an important review for education researchers and policy analysts and help direct future education research efforts in Shanghai.

CHAPTER 1

Overview of Shanghai and Its Education System

Introduction

Located on the eastern shore of China, Shanghai is the country's most populous city, inhabited by 23 million people as of 2013. Administratively, Shanghai has been granted provincial status (along with Beijing, Guangzhou, and Chongqing). As a province Shanghai is divided into 16 county-level divisions or districts. Even though every district has its own urban core, a few districts collectively form the main city while the others form the suburban part, composed of satellite towns and rural areas farther away from the urban core.

Since the Chinese government shifted to more open economic policies in 1978, Shanghai has become one of the largest economic centers in China, with annual GDP per capita close to US$12,000, nearing the World Bank's high-income threshold. The manufacturing and services sectors contribute 48 percent and 51 percent, respectively, to the city's overall economy; agriculture contributes barely 1 percent.

In 2010, the Port of Shanghai overtook the Port of Singapore to become the world's busiest container port. In 2014, the Port of Shanghai set a historic record by handling more than 35 million containers. Shanghai has already set its mid- and long-term development goals: to build the city into one of the finest economic, finance, trade, and shipping centers in the world and to realize its vision of becoming a modern socialist international metropolis by 2020. Shanghai also leads the nation in educational achievement—19 percent of the adult population possess higher education degrees and another 26 percent have attained high school education, as compared with 8.9 percent and 14 percent nationwide.[1]

China has a centralized leadership structure but a decentralized government administration system, delicately balancing the authority of the central government with the autonomy and flexibility of local administration. The central Ministry of Education is responsible for education nationwide, in charge of formulating national development goals and plans for education, and for developing guidelines and policies in all educational domains and monitoring their implementation. However, provinces and municipalities, including Shanghai, maintain a relatively high level of autonomy for developing localized policies, implementation and financing strategies, and province-specific goals and targets. A centerpiece of decentralization is education financing. In the 1980s, the Chinese government reformed education financing from a centralized system with a narrow revenue base to a decentralized system with a diversified and larger revenue system. With the guidance of upper-level educational committees and bureaus, county-level governments became responsible for the financing of compulsory education. The decentralized education financing policy is at the heart of the education outcome disparities between provinces and between rural and urban areas (Ngok 2007).

Education affairs in Shanghai are managed by the Shanghai Municipal Education Commission, under the Chinese Ministry of Education. As shown in figure 1.1, the Shanghai Municipal Education Commission shoulders the major responsibility for educational affairs in Shanghai, in particular the financing and provision of affiliated institutions of higher education. Although a few key higher education institutes are directly financed and managed by the central Ministry of Education, most of Shanghai's universities and colleges are financed and managed by the Shanghai Municipal Education Commission. At the same time,

Figure 1.1 Shanghai Education Management

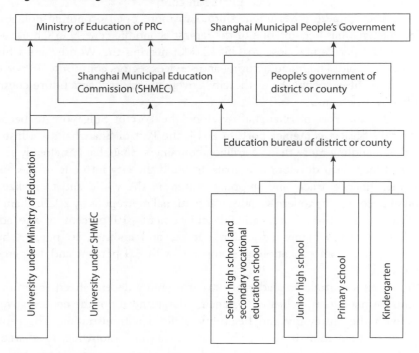

Note: PRC = People's Republic of China.

district (in urban areas) and county (in rural areas) governments are responsible for the financing and provision of preprimary education, the nine-year basic education, and senior secondary education.

Figure 1.2 illustrates the educational structure in Shanghai. Basic education (also known as compulsory education in China) includes primary education (first through fifth grades) and secondary education (sixth through ninth grades).[2] Shanghai's education system has evolved to be the best in the nation in access, equity, and quality. Enrollment in the nine-year basic education has remained about 99.9 percent in the past few years, slightly higher than the national average of 99.7 percent. The promotion rate among junior middle graduates was 96 percent in 2013 compared with 91.2 percent nationwide.[3] Among the 1.2 million basic education students, almost 47 percent, or 0.57 million, were migrant children in 2013. Shanghai achieved a remarkable outcome by enrolling 77 percent of those migrant children in neighborhood public schools and the remaining 23 percent in private schools but with the municipal government covering all tuition and fees.

After completing the nine years of compulsory education, Chinese students, including those in Shanghai, are tracked into various streams of senior secondary education programs strictly based on the scores from the junior secondary graduation examination (*zhong kao*). The streams are general academic or vocational.[4] Within the academic track, there are two further types of programs or schools:

Figure 1.2 Shanghai Education Structure

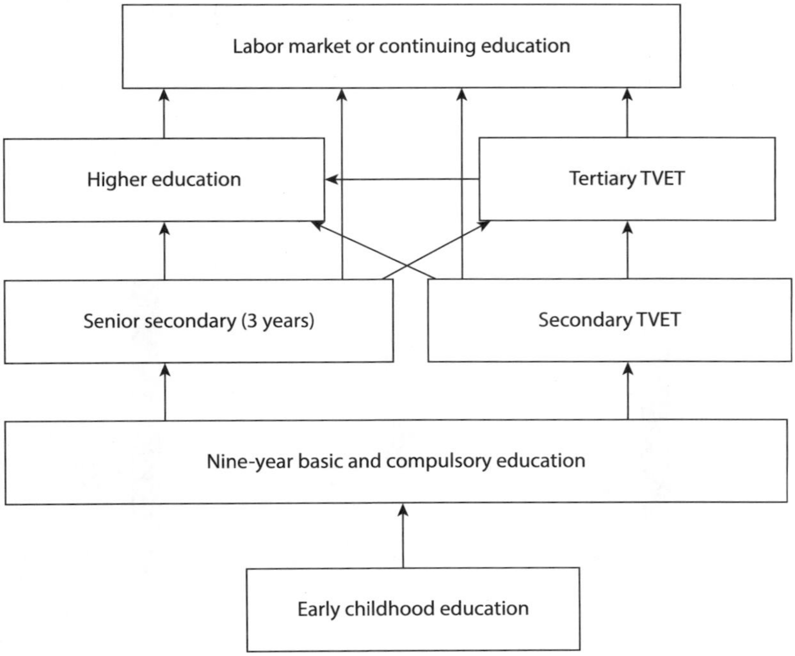

Note: TVET = technical and vocational education training.

the most elite model or experimental senior secondary schools and regular senior secondary schools. Competition is fierce for spots in the model senior secondary schools, which also tend to have the highest proportion of graduates entering the elite and first-tier universities in China or world-class universities abroad.

The government is the dominant financer and provider of education in Shanghai and China, especially in the compulsory education period. Data from the 2012 Programme for International Student Assessment (PISA) confirm that only about 10 percent of regular junior secondary and vocational schools are private.[5] Figure 1.3 presents trends in private enrollment in all levels of education using official data. Private schools that provide compulsory education (within the citizen education track) are nonprofit organizations regulated by the Bureau of Education.[6] They tend to follow the same curriculum as public schools, and most receive government funding in various forms including per student subsidies and teacher training, and they can be eligible for specific project funding.

Table 1.1 presents key information about the size of the Shanghai system and the endowment of teachers. It is important to note that although Shanghai overall has fairly low pupil-to-teacher ratios in preprimary, primary, junior secondary, and even senior secondary education, the average class size is almost triple the pupil-to-teacher ratio. This results from the way teaching and classes are organized. Within each grade there are a number of classroom sections. Each section hosts a group of students that take the same classes and courses with the same teachers and progress to the next grade together. The general basic education subjects include Chinese, math, English, crafts, art, music, physical education, information technology, and natural sciences. In addition, primary school students take ethics and social studies, and secondary school students take science, physics, chemistry, biology, history, geography, fine art, and political science and ethics.

Figure 1.3 Percentage of Private Enrollment in Shanghai by Level and Year

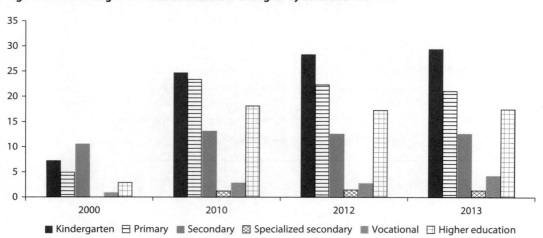

Source: Data from *Shanghai Statistical Yearbook: Education 2014* (http://www.stats-sh.gov.cn/data/toTjnj.xhtml?y=2014e).

Table 1.1 Key Characteristics of Shanghai's Education System, 2014–15

Indicator	Preprimary	Primary	Junior secondary	Senior secondary	Secondary vocational
Number of schools	1,462	757	522	246	104
Number of classes	16,468	20,491	20,491	12,455	4,565
Number of full-time teachers	51,022	41,366	36,049	14,272	8,358
Student enrollment	501,030	792,476	436,696	156,817	153,298
Student-to-teacher ratio	10	19	12	11	18
Average class size	30	39	35	34	—
Gross enrollment ratio, Shanghai (percent)	99.0	99.9	99.9	96.0	—
Gross enrollment ratio, China (percent)	67.5	99.7	104	86.0	—

Note: — = not available.

As in most other Asian countries, segregation of curriculum and pedagogy by subject is the norm and one of the key characteristics of the Chinese education system and philosophy. School children, beginning in first grade, are taught by teachers who are trained and recruited by subject. Each key subject teacher is responsible for teaching that subject. Depending on the school, teachers might be teaching different classes in the same grade or different classes across grades, but only in one subject. However, teachers of noncore subjects such as music, arts, and information technology could teach more subjects.

In 2009 Shanghai participated for the first time in the Organisation for Economic Co-operation and Development's (OECD's) PISA and ranked first in all three subjects (math, reading, and science) (OECD 2009). In 2012, Shanghai continued to be the top performer (OECD 2014). Its mean mathematics score of 613 points, representing a 4.2 percent annualized increase from 2009, is 119 points above the OECD average, the equivalent of nearly three years of schooling. Its mean score of 570 points in reading represents annualized improvement of 4.6 percent since 2009, the equivalent of more than a year-and-a-half of schooling above the OECD average of 496 points. Its mean score in science, 580, is more than three-quarters of a proficiency level above the OECD average of 501. Furthermore, Shanghai is also home to the largest proportion of top performers (proficient at level 5 or 6) in mathematics (55.4 percent), reading (25.1 percent), and science (27.2 percent). With 55.4 percent of students attaining level 5 or 6 in mathematics, Shanghai is the only PISA participant with more students at these top levels than in any other level (table 1.2).

Moreover, Shanghai has one of the most equal education systems among PISA participants. For example, it has the highest proportion of resilient students (19.2 percent), that is, disadvantaged students who perform among the top 25 percent of students across all participating countries and economies after controlling for socioeconomic status. The strength of the relationship between mathematics performance and socioeconomic status is also below the OECD average.

Table 1.2 Snapshot of Performance on PISA 2012 in Math, Reading, and Science in Shanghai and OECD Average

	Indicators	Shanghai	OECD average
Mathematics	Mean score	613	494
	Share of low achievers (below level 2) (percent)	3.8	23.0
	Share of top performers (level 5 or 6) (percent)	55.4	12.6
	Annualized change in score points (2009–12)	4.2	−0.3
Reading	Mean score	570	496
	Annualized change in score points (2009–12)	4.6	0.3
Science	Mean score	580	501
	Annualized change in score points (2009–12)	1.8	0.5

Source: Data from OECD 2014.
Note: The annualized change is the average annual change in PISA score points from a country's/economy's earliest participation in PISA to PISA 2012. It is calculated taking into account all of a country's/economy's participation in PISA. OECD = Organisation for Economic Co-operation and Development; PISA = Programme for International Student Assessment.

Education Development in Shanghai

Shanghai has a history of constant renewal and has been a national champion of various reforms, including in education. Ever since China opened up to the world in the mid-nineteenth century, when western missionaries started to establish western-style schools, Shanghai has been at the forefront of a relentless crusade to update its education system and policies in line with its social and economic development. Table 1A.1 describes the main stages of the evolution of the development of education in Shanghai. The beginning of socialism in China in 1949 laid the foundation for public education for all and emphasized the cultivation of skills to help build the new socialist country. After the unfortunate disintegration of education during the decade-long Cultural Revolution, the Chinese government vowed to resuscitate education and has called for rounds of education reform during the past three decades to bring education in line with the requirements of modern Chinese society. Three strategic documents so far have guided the overall direction of reform: (1) the 1988 State Council "Decisions about Education System Reform," (2) the 1999 State Council "Decisions on Deepening Education Reform and Promoting Quality-Oriented Education in an All-Round Way," and (3) the 2010 State Council "China's Medium- and Long-Term Education Reform and Development Plan Outline." Shanghai has closely followed the central government's reform guidance and has been driving education reform accordingly, becoming a national champion of education innovation.

Shanghai is now beginning to undertake a "Comprehensive Education Reform" as one of the pilot cities in China. This phase of education reform will entail policies that would further emphasize bridging the quality and access gap and promoting child-centered teaching and learning, the innovation and creativity needed for developing 21st-century skills, and lifelong learning.

Annex 1A

Table 1A.1 Development Phases for Shanghai's Basic Educational Reforms (19th Century to Present)

Phases	Key national events	Shanghai impact and activities	Outcomes
The beginning of western influence on Shanghai education (1843–1949)	• Treaty of Nanking (1842): International trading relations • Self-Strengthening Movement (1861–95): Adoption of western knowledge and skills • War of Resistance against Japan (1928–45)	• International influence on local education practices • New-style schools set up by western missionaries • Teacher training institutions emerge in Shanghai • By 1940s, an independent system created by missionaries • Shanghai implements the national education system (1945–49)	• Emergence of a multidimensional structure of education • Institutionalization of teacher training • Cross-learning and translations of western literature in Chinese scripts
Expansion of mass schooling (1949–66)	• The People's Republic of China (PRC) founded in 1949	• More than 20 new higher education institutions (including two normal universities for teacher training) set up • Several new schools set up under the first five-year plan • Vocational education introduced for agricultural communities and manufacturing industry	• Initiation of a public education system for all citizens • Popularization of education among the working class • Cultivation of experts and engineers with higher education for the new republic
A period of educational disintegration (1966–76)	• "The Cultural Revolution" • Education viewed as a means of political indoctrination • Centralized planning	• Several conventional schools and colleges closed down • Students, teachers, and intellectuals sent to villages to be "re-educated" in Maoist theories and lifestyle • Historical scriptures and cultural relics destroyed • Curriculum and administration controlled centrally	• Reversal of educational progress • Educational deprivation for an entire generation • Stifling of diversity and educational innovation • Loss in secondary and higher education
Structural rehabilitation, reorientation, and expansion of education (1977–99)	• Establishment of the National Education Committee (1985) • Decentralization and marketization • *Key policies:* Compulsory Education Law (1986); Decisions about Education System Reform (1988); The Program for Educational Reform and Development in China (1993); Teachers Law of the PRC (1993); Education Law (1995); Vocational Law (1996); Higher Education Law (1998)	• The *Qingpu* experiment (1977–92): Focused on improving teaching method in mathematics; was successful in raising students' performance; later extended to other subjects, and influenced teaching-learning practices nationally • Shanghai becomes the first city to achieve universal primary and secondary education (1985) • Shanghai assumes greater local control over education • Local curriculum reform era I (1986–97): Focused on textbook content, subject categories, pedagogy, disciplinary approach, and assessment orientation	• Nationwide drive to learn and teach • Legalization of various educational provisions • Devolution of power to local authorities • Education linked with economic modernization • Universalization of nine-year school completion • Popularization of general and vocational higher education • Move away from standardized national textbooks to experimentation and diversity • Emergence of Shanghai as an educational model

table continues next page

Table 1A.1 Development Phases for Shanghai's Basic Educational Reforms (19th Century to Present) *(continued)*

Phases	Key national events	Shanghai impact and activities	Outcomes
Quality and equity orientation (1999–2009)	• Decisions on Deepening Education Reform and Promoting Quality-Oriented Education in an All-Round Way (1999) • The Decision about Reform and Development on Basic Education (2001) • The Decision about Further Strengthening Education Work in Rural Areas (2001) • Revised Compulsory Education Law of the PRC (2006)	• Local curriculum reform era II (1999–2007): Elaborated on student-centered and lifelong learning, initiative taking and practical ability, and basic principles of curriculum reform with sufficient autonomy for individual schools • An elaborate construction criterion released for primary and secondary schools in Shanghai (2004) • Large-scale off-school tutoring prohibited (2006) • An evaluation schedule for primary and secondary students' comprehensive ability released in Shanghai (2006) • Policies to promote educational equity in the suburbs (2007) • Shanghai participates in 2009 PISA, and tops the rankings	• Overall revitalization of the education system: educational thought, systems, content, and methods • Weakening of previous obsession with examinations • Revision of learning styles; move away from subject-centered rote learning to integrated problem solving • Emphasis on equity and quality of educational opportunity for rural and migrant populations • Achievement of almost universal (99.7 percent) primary and secondary education in 2009 • Generation of international attention for Shanghai's educational achievement and practices
For the lifelong development of every student (2010–present)	• The release of the Outline of National Medium- and Long-Term Education Reform and Development Plan (2010) • The ratio of education expenditure to GDP reaches 4 percent (2012) • Promotion of the separation of administration, running, and evaluation in education domain from the government's functions (2015)	• The joint construction of National Education Comprehensive Reform Base between Shanghai municipality and the central government (2010): To speed up modernization process of Shanghai education, via strengthening of local ability to support national strategies • Criterion for running compulsory schools released (2011) • Green Indicators of Academic Quality of Primary and Secondary School Students released (2011) • Shanghai tops the rankings in PISA 2012, again • Notice for executing pilot construction of school-based educational quality guarantee system, Shanghai (2015)	• Acknowledgment of the issues of cultural diversity; students' individual requirements; and teachers' work, professional development, and life quality • Expansion of policies to strengthen weak schools • Transformation of the government's administrative functions from detailed guidance to evaluations, to emphasizing school autonomy and accountability • Development of high-quality tertiary and vocational skill and information and communications technology programs • Rise in interest in developing Shanghai and China as competitive global education models

Note: PISA = Programme for International Student Assessment.

Notes

1. National Bureau of Statistics of China 2013 (http://data.stats.gov.cn/easyquery.htm ?cn=C01&zb=A0306&sj=2010).

2. China's educational structure consists of six years of primary education, three years of junior secondary education, and another three years of senior secondary education.

3. *China Statistical Yearbook: Education 2013* (http://www.stats.gov.cn/tjsj/ndsj/2013 /indexeh.htm).

4. The Chinese government has issued guidance to maintain an enrollment ratio of 1:1 in academic vs. vocational secondary schools.

5. Private education literally translates into "managed by people" in Chinese to deemphasize the profit nature of pure private education.

6. A number of international schools or schools established by other countries, such as the German or American schools, are in operation and admit only non-Chinese students; these schools are considered outside of citizen education and are not subject to oversight by the county or district Bureaus of Education.

References

Ngok, K. 2007. "Chinese Education Policy in the Context of Decentralization and Marketization: Evolution and Implications." *Asia Pacific Education Review* 8 (1): 142– 57. http://files.eric.ed.gov/fulltext/EJ768972.pdf

OECD (Organisation for Economic Co-operation and Development). 2009. "PISA 2009 Executive Summary." OECD Paris. http://www.oecd.org/pisa/pisaproducts /46619703.pdf.

———. 2014. *PISA 2012 Results in Focus: What 15-Year-Olds Know and What They Can Do with What They Know.* Paris: OECD Publishing. http://www.oecd.org/pisa /keyfindings/pisa-2012-results-overview.pdf.

CHAPTER 2

Systems Approach to Analyzing Education Policies and Linking Them to Implementation and Learning Outcomes

Introduction

The main guiding principles for the background studies and this report are the World Bank's Systems Approach for Better Education Results (SABER) and further linking of policies to implementation and learning outcomes. Too often education systems and policies are partitioned separately into, for example, teachers, financing, curriculum, assessment, and so on, without attempting to bring them together. Although not completely, the report adopts the SABER tools for collecting information on policy and institutions in multiple domains including teachers, school financing, school autonomy and accountability, assessment, and private provision in education, so as to form a comprehensive picture of the basic education system in Shanghai.

Another common tendency for education policy analysis is to examine the various education inputs and attempt to link them with learning outcomes. This approach has been heavily influenced by the education production philosophy and tends to ignore the complicated education process that happens within classrooms and within every student-teacher interaction. This report attempts to fill some part of the education black box by collecting information on policies and institutions, as well as information on the extent to which the policies have been implemented at the school level, and then linking this information with learning outcomes as measured in the Programme for International Assessment (PISA) (figure 2.1). In this way, efforts were made to link performance with the specific practices and policies that mediate between mere inputs and outcomes and that may be replicated in other settings or countries.

Figure 2.1 The Black Box of Education Production

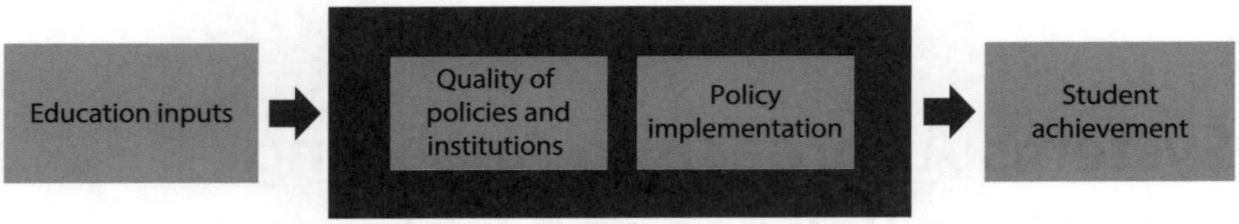

Source: Adapted from Rogers 2015.

Measuring Policy Intent and the SABER Instruments

Efforts to collect and document policy information for specific country education systems are numerous. However, consistent criteria for data collection are
absent, nor is there a common framework that would allow policies to be compared and benchmarked against "good practices." Researchers and policy makers
often find themselves in a sea of policy information and have to rely on their own
knowledge and experience to interpret the data and come up with recommendations. Recently the World Bank Education Global Practice developed SABER—
the Systems Approach for Better Education Results—as a policy information
collection and diagnostic tool for analyzing and comparing the different policy domains of education systems across the globe. SABER is primarily used
to measure expressed and explicit policy intent, usually based on official and
published policy information. The existing set of SABER modules include those
presented in figure 2.2.

Of the set of policy domains in figure 2.2, early childhood development,
teachers, school finance, school autonomy and accountability, and student assessment were selected for this report's in-depth assessment in Shanghai. Early childhood development was later excluded from this report because basic education
in China (and thus in Shanghai) is defined to include only the six years of primary education and three years of junior secondary education. A separate China
and Shanghai SABER on early childhood development will be produced.

Each SABER module has a number of policy goals that are backed by a thorough review of education research evidence to date on what matters for education. Each policy goal is further broken down into a number of policy levers, that
is, specific policy actions that the government can take to achieve the policy
goals. All the data in this report were collected in Shanghai using the SABER data
collection instruments to ensure comparability with other education systems.
Data collection instruments comprise a set of specific indicators constructed to
measure to what extent each policy lever has been achieved.

A scoring rubric is used to analyze the policy data collected and further clas-
sify each policy lever into four levels—latent, emerging, established, and
advanced (table 2.1). A "latent" score signifies that the policy behind the indicator is not yet in place or that there is limited engagement in developing the
related education policy. An "emerging" score indicates that the policy in place

Figure 2.2 SABER Domains or Policy Areas

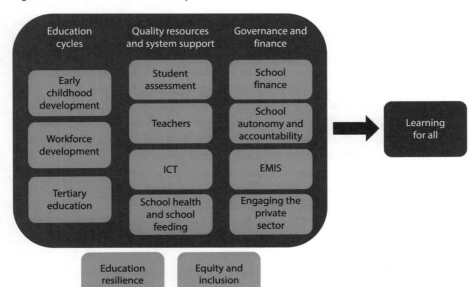

Source: Abdul-Hamid 2014.
Note: EMIS = education management information system; ICT = information and communications technology;
SABER = Systems Approach for Better Education Results.

Table 2.1 SABER Scoring Rubric

Latent ●○○○	*Emerging* ●●○○	*Established* ●●●○	*Advanced* ●●●●
Reflects policy is not in place, or limited engagement	Reflects some good practices; policy work still in progress	Reflects good practices, with some limitations	Reflects international best practices

Note: SABER = Systems Approach for Better Education Results.

reflects some good practices but that policy development is still in progress. An "established" score indicates that the program or policy reflects good practices and meets the minimum standards but may be limited in its content and scope. An "advanced" score indicates that the program or policy reflects best practices and can be considered on par with international standards.

Each chapter that follows is organized according to the specific SABER goals included in the policy domain. The rating attached to each goal has been fully discussed and verified with the respective SABER teams and adheres strictly to the rubric for scoring the particular goal. Whenever applicable, data collected from the school surveys were used to shed light on implementation of these policies, that is, the extent to which the government's policy intent has been translated into school-level implementation.

Measuring Policy Implementation

In many countries, policy intent or statements are not always implemented because of various constraints such as lack of resources, capacity, or political will. In some low-income countries, the gap between policy and implementation can be quite large. Measuring the extent to which policies are implemented, especially at the school level, will establish a stronger link between policies and student learning outcomes. Therefore, in addition to assessing education policies using the SABER modules, the report makes serious efforts to collect data and use existing studies to substantiate the extent to which official policies are indeed being implemented at school or even classroom levels.

Most relevantly, the team designed questionnaires and collaborated with Shanghai Normal University to develop and administer a survey to 153 school principals to understand education practices in relationship to the policy goals under each SABER module. The sample of 153 schools comprises junior secondary schools that participated in both the 2009 and 2012 PISA. PISA adopts a random sampling strategy to select a sample of schools and students representative of the participating country's or region's student body. Therefore, the results from this 153-school survey can be said to be reflective of education practices in Shanghai.

Additional data and information were gleaned from existing studies, both Chinese and international, on the efficacy of specific policies, though most tend to have very small samples. For example, education expenditure data were used along with information on teacher salaries from labor force surveys. Studies related to the school-level teaching-research group were also referenced to highlight the important practice of school-level professional development.

Connecting Policy Intent, Implementation, and PISA Learning Outcome Measures

A further step toward better understanding policy impacts is to link policies and implementation with student learning outcomes. Rigorous impact evaluations are rare, unfortunately. This report draws on PISA 2009 and PISA 2012 cross-sectional data to investigate which school-level characteristics (both policies and practices) are associated with the mathematical, reading, and scientific literacy and problem-solving skills of 15-year-olds in Shanghai. In particular, the report addresses the way in which different school characteristics are associated with students' mathematical, reading, and scientific literacy. For each program (lower secondary, upper secondary general, and upper secondary vocational), PISA scores on the three domains are subjected to a regression estimation using school characteristics, and controlling for individual and family background characteristics. Furthermore, because Shanghai aims to develop into a globally competitive city with a young generation of innovative and critical thinkers with strong problem-solving skills, the analysis also took advantage of the new problem-solving module in the 2012 PISA to examine the impact of family and school characteristics on students' problem-solving skills. In this way, the report attempts to establish an analytical loop connecting policies, implementation, and student outcomes.

Limitations of the Study

The limitations of this study need to be acknowledged up front. The PISA and SABER instruments employed for this study, put together, measure only a few segments of the complex and multilayered system of education in Shanghai. PISA measures students in the school system only on their academic performance, and only on a select few subjects and competencies. Similarly, the SABER instruments are intended to assess the policy and institutional environment and diagnose areas for improvement. Neither of these instruments fully capture the intricacies of Shanghai's current educational systems and processes. To overcome this limitation, effort has been made to supplement information through surveys with school principals, interviews with key education thinkers in Shanghai, and detailed discussions with officials on the Shanghai Municipal Education Commission. However, it must be noted that principal surveys ($N = 153$), though sampled randomly to be representative of the population in Shanghai, were administered through self-reporting and hence are subject to associated biases.

Additional limitation comes from the existing overlaps in the policy goals and indicators measured in different SABER modules, namely SABER–Teachers, SABER–Finance, SABER–School Autonomy and Accountability, and SABER–Student Assessment. These overlaps have led to associated repetition in documentation of findings, as is evident in subsequent chapters of this report. Nevertheless, this exercise has allowed us to comprehensively look at issues through multiple policy lenses.

References

Abdul-Hamid, Husein. 2014. "What Matters Most for Education Management Information Systems: A Framework Paper." SABER Working Paper 7, World Bank, Washington, DC. http://wbgfiles.worldbank.org/documents/hdn/ed/saber/supporting_doc /Background/EMIS/Framework_SABER-EMIS.pdf.

Rogers, H. 2015. "Tools to Measure Teacher Performance and Skills." World Bank, Washington, DC. http://www.worldbank.org/content/dam/Worldbank/Event/ECA /central-asia/1%20Tools%20for%20measuring%20teacher%20performance __Halsey%20Rogers__Bishkek.pdf.

CHAPTER 3

Attracting and Developing an Excellent Teaching Force

Introduction

Teachers undisputedly constitute the most important input in education. It is no exaggeration to say that any time a student and a teacher interact some learning is taking place. This report uses the Systems Approach for Better Education Results (SABER) teacher module (SABER–Teachers) to collect and analyze policy and institution data on 10 core teacher policy areas (see box 3.1). The policy data from SABER are complemented with data gathered through principal surveys ($N = 153$), key informant interviews with teachers and education officials of the Shanghai Municipal Education Commission, and review of diverse policy and research literature.

SABER–Teachers analyzes the teacher policy data collected in the 10 areas in box 3.1 to assess each system's progress in achieving eight teacher policy goals (see figure 3.1): (1) setting clear expectations for teachers, (2) attracting the best into teaching, (3) preparing teachers with useful training and experience, (4) matching teachers' skills with students' needs, (5) leading teachers with strong principals, (6) monitoring teaching and learning, (7) supporting teachers to improve instruction, and (8) motivating teachers to perform. World Bank (2013) offers greater details on SABER–Teachers and the evidence base for the instrument design.

Overall, as demonstrated in table 3.1, it has been ascertained on the basis of SABER–Teachers that Shanghai's policy environment for teachers can be scored between "established" and "advanced."

Policy Goal 1: Setting Clear Expectations for Teachers (Advanced)

Shanghai has clear standards for student achievement. The "Municipal Primary and Secondary School Curriculum Plan" provides overall guidelines on learning objectives, curriculum structure, standards for curriculum design, learning materials, and evaluation across all subjects from first grade to twelfth grade

Box 3.1 Teacher Policy Areas for Data Collection under SABER–Teachers

1. Requirements to enter and remain in teaching
2. Initial teacher education
3. Recruitment and employment
4. Teachers' workload and autonomy
5. Professional development
6. Compensation (salary and nonsalary benefits)
7. Retirement rules and benefits
8. Monitoring and evaluation of teacher quality
9. Teacher representation and voice
10. School leadership

Source: World Bank 2013.

Figure 3.1 Eight Teacher Policy Goals under SABER–Teachers

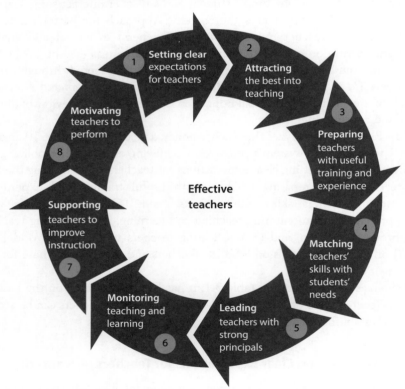

Source: World Bank 2013.

Table 3.1 SABER–Teachers Scoring, Shanghai, 2015

Policy and resource framework (Goals and indicators)	SABER score
Setting clear expectations for teachers	●●●●
1. Setting clear expectations regarding student learning and official tasks	●●●○
2. Providing useful guidance on the use of teachers' work hours	●●●●
Attracting the best into teaching	●●●●
1. Ensuring entry requirements to attract talented candidates	●●●○
2. Offering competitive pay	●●●●
3. Ensuring appealing work conditions	●●●●
4. Offering attractive career opportunities	●●●●
Preparing teachers with useful training and experience	●●●○
1. Ensuring minimum standards for preservice teacher training programs	●●●○
2. Ensuring that teacher entrants are familiar with classroom practices	●●●●
Matching teachers' skills with students' needs	●●●○
1. Providing incentives for teachers to work in hard-to-staff schools	●●●●
2. Providing incentives for teachers to teach critical shortage subjects	●●●○
Leading teachers with strong principals	●●●○
1. Investing in the development of qualified school leaders	●●●●
2. Expecting principals to support and improve instructional practice	●●●○
Monitoring teaching and learning	●●●●
1. Ensuring data on student achievement are available to inform teaching and policy	●●●○
2. Setting systems to assess and monitor teacher performance	●●●○
3. Providing multiple mechanisms to evaluate teacher performance	●●●●
Supporting teachers to improve instruction	●●●○
1. Providing opportunities for professional development	●●●○
2. Ensuring that professional development activities are collaborative and focus on instructional improvement	●●●●
3. Ensuring that professional development is based on perceived needs	●●●○
Motivating teachers to perform	●●●○
1. Linking career opportunities to performance	●●●○
2. Providing mechanisms to hold teachers accountable	●●●○
3. Linking teacher compensation to performance	●●●○

Note: Scoring rubric: Latent (●○○○), Emerging (●●○○), Established (●●●○), Advanced (●●●●).
SABER = Systems Approach for Better Education Results.

in Shanghai. Furthermore, for each subject, the city has released curriculum standards that specify the knowledge areas and skills students need to acquire every year.

Table 3.2 provides an example of learning objectives for first and second grade Chinese. It demonstrates that the objectives include both quantifiable indicators (for example, recognize approximately 2,000 common Chinese characters and write 1,000 characters) and descriptions of competencies. Similarly, table 3.3 shows selected objectives for first and second grade math. The curriculum standards serve as important references that align teachers' daily work with students' academic achievement.

Table 3.2 Selected Learning Objectives for First and Second Grade Chinese

By the end of second grade, students will be able to

1. Read Pinyin[a] correctly; know how to use a dictionary; recognize approximately 2,000 common Chinese characters and write 1,000 characters
2. Understand textbook content; express opinion after reading passages
3. Listen to other people carefully and communicate actively
4. Write several complete sentences to express opinion
5. Participate in activities at the class, school, and community level

Source: Shanghai Municipal Education Commission 2005.
a. Pinyin is the standard system of Romanized spelling to transcribe the Mandarin pronunciations of Chinese characters.

Table 3.3 Selected Learning Objectives for First and Second Grade Math

By the end of second grade, students will be able to

1. Understand and compare numbers; add, subtract, multiply, and divide; make estimates
2. Solve simple math equations and apply to practical problems
3. Calculate the circumference and area of various shapes
4. Understand statistical charts and perform simple analysis such as calculating the mean

Source: Shanghai Municipal Education Commission 2005.

As an illustration of how the curriculum standards are achieved, the survey of principals (see chapter 2) confirms that 90 percent of the schools surveyed require teachers to design detailed teacher lesson plans based on the standards and supervise the implementation status of the teaching plans. In addition, 81 percent of the schools regularly organize teachers to attend workshops to study the curriculum standards for their subjects.

There are explicit expectations for teachers' tasks. The Teachers Law of the People's Republic of China 1993 (hereinafter referred to as the Teachers Law) defines the general obligations of teachers. At the provincial level, not only should teachers fulfill teaching contracts and carry out the school teaching plan suggested by the Shanghai Municipal Education Commission (table 3.4), but they should also dedicate themselves to the moral, physical, and intellectual development of students and organize relevant learning activities for students. Teachers are also expected to improve their own moral ethics and pedagogical expertise. In Shanghai, teachers' responsibilities extend beyond the classroom and encompass both extracurricular activities and professional development.

The official working time for teachers is eight hours every day for five days a week, including both teaching and nonteaching hours. Overtime hours worked during the weekend are compensated. The education system in Shanghai clearly recognizes the need for teachers to spend time outside the classroom. On average, teachers in Shanghai report spending 14 hours per week on actual teaching, that is, more than 5 hours less than the Teaching and Learning International Survey (TALIS) 2013–14 average of 19.3 hours per week (figure 3.2). However, teachers in Shanghai report spending more time per week than in other TALIS

Table 3.4 Teaching Time by Subject, Primary Education

Subject	Teaching time
Chinese, math, and English	35 min./class × 15 classes per week (first and second grades)
	35 min./class × 13 classes per week (third through sixth grades)
Music, physical education, and arts	35 min./class × 18 classes per week
Other subjects	35 min./class × 16 classes per week

Source: Shanghai Municipal Education Commission 2005.

Figure 3.2 Distribution of Working Hours Spent on Various Teaching and Nonteaching Activities

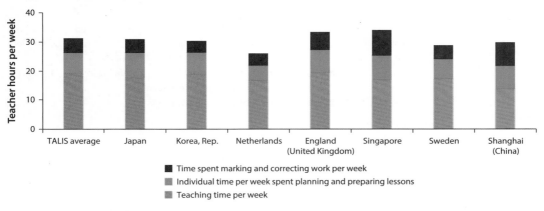

■ Time spent marking and correcting work per week
■ Individual time per week spent planning and preparing lessons
■ Teaching time per week

Sources: Data from OECD 2013, 2014.
Note: TALIS = Teaching and Learning International Survey.

countries on planning their lessons and student counselling (OECD 2014). Additionally, teachers in Shanghai seem to spend relatively less time, 8 percent of their total class time, on keeping order in the classroom compared with the TALIS 2013–14 average of 12 percent of class time (figure 3.3). Overall, it has been estimated that despite the relatively fewer number of hours spent on teaching per week, the great majority of teachers' class time in Shanghai is spent on actual teaching and learning, 86 percent compared with the TALIS 2013–14 average of 79 percent (OECD 2014).

Nationally, the "Provisions for Rewarding Teachers and Educators" (1998), released by the Ministry of Education, guide teachers and provide them with incentives to engage in curriculum design, school plan development, and research activities. Teachers with outstanding achievement in both teaching and nonteaching tasks are honored with the title of "model teacher" and a monetary reward. At the city level, regulations stipulate that teachers should spend time on instructional improvement to strengthen subject knowledge and pedagogy.

Figure 3.3 Distribution of Weekly Class Time Spent on Various Teaching and Nonteaching Activities

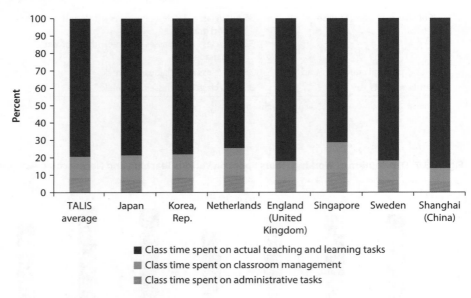

Class time spent on actual teaching and learning tasks
Class time spent on classroom management
Class time spent on administrative tasks

Sources: Data from OECD 2013, 2014.
Note: TALIS = Teaching and Learning International Survey.

Policy Goal 2: Attracting the Best into Teaching (Advanced)

Teaching is a well-regarded profession in Shanghai with an established set of entry requirements. Primary school teachers need to have at least a three-year tertiary college degree (*da zhuan*, equivalent to the International Standard Classification of Education [ISCED] 5B level) and secondary teachers need to have at least a four-year bachelor's degree (equivalent to the ISCED 5A level). In addition to the academic requirements, all candidates must pass a written test to obtain the teacher certificate to be eligible to teach in primary and secondary schools in Shanghai. In the recruitment process at the school level, candidates participate in interviews and a mock teaching assessment during which they teach a mini lesson to demonstrate their teaching competencies. Over the years competition for teaching positions in Shanghai has become fierce. A Shanghai teacher job fair held in the winter of 2014 confirmed that even a master's degree from an elite or overseas university is no guarantee that the candidate will be able to land a job. Schools and principals tend to put high priority on pedagogical skills.

To attract even more candidates to the teaching profession, Shanghai provides multiple pathways into teaching. One pathway is through the teacher preparation programs at three-year or four-year tertiary institutions. Those training programs equip students with subject knowledge, pedagogical skills, and some practical experience inside the classroom (commonly six months' practice before graduation). Students graduate with a teaching degree and make up a significant proportion of the candidates for the profession. In addition, anyone who has the minimum educational qualification and successfully obtains the teacher certificate can apply to be a teacher (see box 3.2). Those pathways allow for more flexible entry points, so that both recent graduates and talented professionals have the opportunity to become teachers. Among the 153 schools surveyed, on average, 85 percent of teachers were graduates of teacher preparation programs.

The central government also provides incentives to increase the pool of teaching candidates and encourage teacher retention. Since 2007, six nationally affiliated teacher preparation colleges have offered free tuition and living stipends to teacher candidates who agree to stay in the teaching profession for more than 10 years after graduation (at least 2 years in rural areas). Shanghai in particular launched two talent recruitment plans in 2014 to proactively recruit high-quality candidates who do not necessarily have a teaching degree: one plan recruits candidates from Shanghai's four top universities, and the other hosts teacher recruitment fairs in Beijing's top universities to encourage candidates to come to Shanghai.

Teacher pay is appealing and varies according to performance and years of service. In Shanghai, the common perception of the teaching profession is that it is a financially stable, middle-class career. Indeed, the Teachers Law stipulates that

---

Box 3.2 Obtaining a Teacher Certificate

The process of obtaining a teacher certificate in China underwent major changes in 2012. Before 2012, the process differed based on the candidate's academic background. Candidates from teacher preparation programs at three-year or four-year tertiary institutions needed to fulfill two requirements to receive the certificate upon graduation: pass the exams for education studies and education psychology studies and obtain a certificate of proficiency in speaking Mandarin. Candidates from other tertiary programs (nonteaching) needed to fulfill one additional requirement: pass a 30-minute subject-specific mock teaching session (15 minutes of teaching and 15 minutes of interview) conducted by the local education commission.

In 2012, Shanghai was selected to pilot the national teacher certificate reform. All eligible candidates now need to pass a national exam to receive the certificate. The exam consists of a written section and a subject-specific interview. For basic education, the written exam includes two subjects: (1) comprehensives, covering teaching philosophy, education laws and regulations, ethics, cultural literacy, and general abilities; and (2) teaching knowledge and abilities, covering the foundation of education, student guidance, classroom management, subject knowledge, class design and implementation, evaluation (primary education only), and psychology (secondary education only). Secondary school teachers also need to participate in a subject-specific examination. Only candidates who have passed the written test can proceed to the interview stage for receiving the certificate.

How Shanghai Does It • http://dx.doi.org/10.1596/978-1-4648-0790-9

teachers' average salary should be equal to or higher than the average salary of civil servants in China. Shanghai's GDP per capita topped RMB 90,100 in 2013, while the average starting salary for new teachers was approximately RMB 80,000, or 89 percent of GDP per capita. This starting salary for new teachers is comparable to that in other countries around the world (table 3.5): in Finland, the average starting salary for new teachers was 89 percent of GDP per capita; in Japan, the rate was 84 percent; the Republic of Korea's new teachers received 113 percent of GDP per capita; while U.S. teachers were paid 79 percent of GDP per capita (OECD 2011a).

The average annual salary for all school-level teachers in Shanghai was RMB 100,472 in 2010, the highest in the nation; the national average was only RMB 37,786 (Shan 2013). A 2014 survey of wages in urban units by employment sector confirmed that the overall education profession (including public and private and all levels from preprimary to senior secondary) has an average wage of RMB 96,165 in Shanghai, which is much higher than the RMB 56,580 average at the national level (China Statistical Yearbook 2015).

In addition to a comfortable and stable salary, permanent full-time teachers are entitled to medical and retirement benefits in Shanghai. Furthermore, Shanghai has introduced a performance pay salary structure that divides the teaching salary into two parts: (1) a base salary that varies according to years of service and teaching rank; teachers with longer years of service, a higher rank (accredited based on evaluations), or extra responsibilities have a higher base salary; and (2) a performance-based salary. The 30 percent of the wage bill dedicated to merit-based awards to teachers is further divided into three components: (1) an occupation-related allowance, set by the Shanghai Bureau of Human Resources and Social Security and the Shanghai Bureau of Finance; (2) a workload allowance, based on the number of classes teachers teach every month and municipal guidelines; and (3) a performance reward. Teachers with outstanding performance during the year receive a higher performance reward.

Nationally, the level of compensation appears less attractive because education financing is primarily the responsibility of local governments. Because local governments vary in fiscal capacity, their capacity to compensate teachers also varies. According to a 2014 national salary survey (China Statistical Yearbook 2015), the average salary of professionals working in the education sector was RMB 56,580, ranking 10th lowest out of 19 sectors and slightly higher than the

Table 3.5 New Teachers' Salary in Comparison with GDP per Capita

Nation or economy	Percent of GDP per capita
Shanghai	89
Finland	89
Japan	84
Korea, Rep.	113
United States	79

Source: OECD 2011a.

national average of RMB 56,360 across all sectors (figure 3.4). Although the education sector encompasses a wide range of professions and positions, these statistics provide a glance into teacher pay at the national level.

Evidence from past research suggests that the compensation package factors into individuals' decisions to become teachers (Boyd et al. 2006; Dolton 1990; Wolter and Denzler 2003). The appealing salary level and benefits in Shanghai aid in attracting new teachers. Furthermore, teachers with outstanding performance and substantial length of service can make several times as much as new teachers do. This salary distribution structure to a certain extent encourages teacher retention and provides incentives to teachers to invest in continuous improvement of their knowledge and skills. However, the actual performance-based incentives that principals have the autonomy to distribute constitute up to 9 percent of total teacher salary. This level of performance reward might not be sufficient to motivate the intended level of outstanding teaching practices.

Working conditions are appealing. All schools in Shanghai must comply with infrastructure standards as a prerequisite for school establishment. Schools also must comply with sanitation standards and are regularly inspected. Primary and secondary schools generally supply each teacher a computer to assist with daily tasks.

Student-to-teacher ratios are also conducive to establishing adequate working conditions in Shanghai. In 2012, the student-teacher ratio was 16:1 for primary schools and 12:1 for secondary schools, on par with other high-performing countries (figure 3.5). The city also sets the maximum ceiling for class size so

Figure 3.4 Average Wage in Various Employment Categories, China, 2013

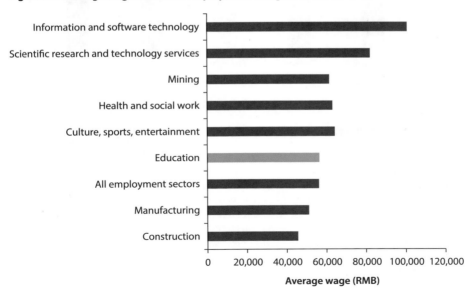

Source: Data from China Statistical Yearbook 2015.

that no class should exceed 40 students. The difference between the student-to-teacher ratio and average class size is due to the way teaching and learning are organized. As in many East Asian countries, teachers in China and Shanghai are trained, recruited, and organized by subject starting from teachers of first grade. Each key subject teacher is responsible for teaching his or her subject specialty.

Career advancement mechanisms are in place to attract qualified individuals to the profession. Teachers can apply for both academic and administrative positions within the school system to assume greater responsibilities. Furthermore, unlike many other systems in which one is either a teacher or not a teacher, teachers have the opportunity to advance professionally throughout their teaching careers through a very explicit five-tier ranking system (table 3.6).

Figure 3.5 Average Student-to-Teacher Ratio for Primary Schools, 2012–13

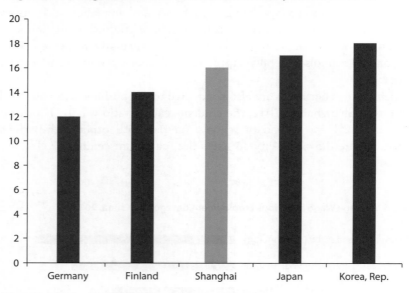

Source: Data from World Bank 2016.

Table 3.6 Tiered Ranking System for Teachers

Rank	Requirements
Third-grade teachers	One to three years of service
Second-grade teachers	Three to five years of service + third-grade teacher rank obtained + school-level internal evaluation
First-grade teachers	At least five years of service + second-grade teacher rank obtained + school-level internal evaluation + district-level external evaluation
Senior-grade teachers	At least five years of service + first-grade teacher rank obtained + school-level internal evaluation + district-level external evaluation
Outstanding teachers	Only granted to teachers with many years of service and outstanding teaching practices

Source: Adapted from Education Bureau of Jiading District of Shanghai 2014.

Under the system, teachers are evaluated regularly for promotion to a higher rank, which is accompanied with a salary increase, based on their years of service and teaching performance. Out of the 153 schools surveyed, 97 percent have established a specific committee to evaluate teachers' qualifications for promotion. A selective number of "outstanding" teachers have been hired as professors in teaching preparation universities to provide practical guidance to teacher candidates. This career ladder provides an effective mechanism to nurture excellent educators and retain them in the teaching profession.

Policy Goal 3: Preparing Teachers with Useful Training and Experience (Established)

The initial education requirement in Shanghai for teacher candidates could be enhanced. Currently, a three-year tertiary education (equivalent to the ISCED 5B level) is required for primary school teachers, and a four-year university education (equivalent to the ISCED 5A level) is required for secondary school teachers. In practice, however, the academic requirement is more stringent. Overall, 97 percent of the schools surveyed have a minimum academic requirement of a four-year bachelor's degree when making hiring decisions. And among the existing teaching force, the survey indicates that 94 percent of teachers already possess bachelor's degree qualifications. The Programme for International Student Assessment (PISA) 2012 Shanghai survey shows that 97.6 percent of teachers have teacher certificates, with very little variation between schools (standard deviation = 16 percent).

Therefore, it is time for Shanghai to make a policy change to reflect the higher entry requirement. Most Organisation for Economic Co-operation and Development (OECD) and high-performing East Asian countries require teacher applicants to have at least a bachelor's degree equivalent to ISCED 5A, as in Korea and Singapore. Finland requires teachers to have a research-oriented master's degree (OECD 2011a).

Opportunities exist for teacher trainees and new teachers to gain classroom experience. Teacher education programs at three-year and four-year tertiary institutions in Shanghai generally have a six-month classroom teaching component built into the curriculum. This preservice classroom experience allows teacher entrants to apply their pedagogical methods and gain concrete skills in classroom management.

According to the survey results, 86 percent of the schools require teachers to have completed two weeks to 24 months of in-classroom teaching as part of their preservice training. Furthermore, all first-year basic education teachers in Shanghai are required to obtain classroom experience through a one-year in-service induction program to facilitate transition to the teaching job and before hiring is finalized. This time also serves as a probationary period. The induction-probation program requires teachers to spend 50 percent of their time teaching in the classroom and 50 percent receiving professional development at district teacher training centers where they receive training on ethics, pedagogy, and student activity design. This program creates a supportive environment for new teachers to share issues they encounter in their first year of teaching and provides targeted training to strengthen their teaching skills. If new teachers do not meet the various requirements during the one-year probation or fail to pass the evaluations organized by the training center and the schools, schools are not obligated to formally hire them. The probationary period also allows new teachers themselves to reflect on the profession and determine if teaching is indeed their calling. They are allowed to not sign a teaching contract if they decide not to become teachers or want to find another school in which to work.

Both during this probationary period and after becoming part of the regular teaching force, teachers become part of the school teaching-research group, which gathers teachers together by subject. These groups frequently engage in various professional and instructional activities such as mentoring, peer coaching, demonstration lessons, preparing lesson plans jointly, and studying new curriculum standards and pedagogy. The structure and activities become integral to a teacher's teaching and work life in school. Details of the teaching-research group are discussed later.

Shanghai teachers generally have a very high level of content knowledge, especially in the core subject areas of math, Chinese, and English. Figure 3.6 shows that the average scores on a teacher test in Chinese, mathematics, and English are, respectively, 105, 110, and 123 out of a possible 150 for a selected sample of rural

Figure 3.6 Teacher Test Scores and Passing Rates in Rural Shanghai

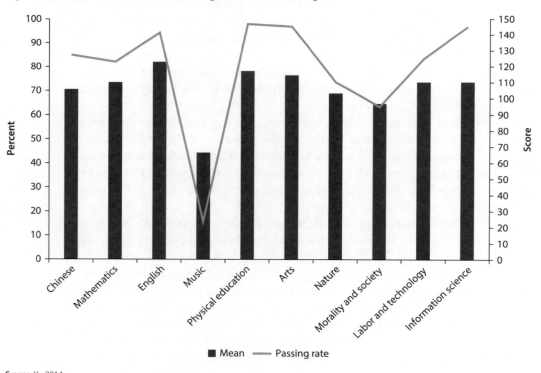

Source: Xu 2014.

teachers in Shanghai. The lowest score is in music, which is not part of the content required for either high school entrance or college entrance (Xu 2014). Urban teachers are expected to have even higher content-related competencies.

Policy Goal 4: Matching Teachers' Skills with Students' Needs (Established)

Shanghai provides teachers and principals with incentives to work in hard-to-staff schools. These schools are usually in the rural and suburban districts where transportation takes much longer and schools admit more migrant and disadvantaged students, conceivably exacerbating inequality in learning outcomes. Recognizing this issue, Shanghai recently launched a number of initiatives to build a stronger teaching and leadership force in the rural districts. Those initiatives center on flexible and temporary transfer or rotation of teachers and administrators with built-in incentives and help leverage the city's resources to serve underprivileged populations and allow struggling schools to catch up (box 3.3).

- Teachers who choose to work at rural schools in Shanghai could receive priority in admission to graduate schools and accreditation of higher teacher ranks, one-time monetary stipends, and compensation.
- Every year about 20 outstanding teachers from central districts are placed in twinning schools in rural or suburban districts.

Box 3.3 An Account of a Teacher's Experience, Jinshan

The Story of Ms. Jinjin Yuan

Ms. Jinjin Yuan is an outstanding teacher from central district who was temporarily transferred to a suburban district of Jinshan. "I was deployed to teach in the Jinshan District, right after being promoted to "outstanding teacher" rank. Most friends considered this an inconvenience and called it "a gift with imperfection." However, after a few months of teaching there, I had gained much professionally from this experience. Furthermore, I could see the changes I was making to the Jinshan early childhood education. This is really a heart-warming gift for me."

Ever since Ms. Yuan was deployed to Jinshan and become the head of the teacher-research group, she has brought with her a wealth of teaching experience to share with the fellow teachers in the new school. She believes that teacher evaluation should not just be based on end-of-the-year tests, but rather should be based on the extent to which the teacher has incorporated the value of "process is more important than outcome" in his or her teaching. She actively encouraged teachers to carefully teach and observe children, and constantly synthesize and reflect on classroom practices. Ms. Yuan quickly gained the trust and respect of other teachers and contributed to a positive culture of teaching and research. More and more teachers would visit Ms. Yuan's office to discuss pedagogy. The Jinshan Bureau of Education founded the "JinJin Teaching Lab." More than 60 teachers applied to be one of the 10 students of the "Lab."

Source: Translated from *China Education Daily* 2015 (http://sc.cqn.com.cn/jiaoyuzhiliang/280476.html).

- A system of principal rotation has been set up; in 2013, the city deployed nine skilled principals from central districts to schools in the rural districts to serve as mentors and offer management advice for two years.
- "Senior-grade" teachers that choose to teach in rural districts can receive an extension of retirement of one to five years.

The transfer of teachers across schools is relatively rare in Shanghai. Changing schools is usually at the teacher's own initiative, in which case the teacher will go through the same recruitment process as new teachers, including an evaluation of credentials and past teaching performance.

Overall, Shanghai has not faced any critical shortage of teachers in any particular subjects in basic education, partly thanks to the steady stream of teacher entrants from teacher preparation programs and other pathways. Furthermore, schools have different levels of autonomy in hiring teachers based on their individual demand. Hiring practices differ across districts. In some districts, schools can post positions directly. However, candidates still need to take and pass the district-level exam to be eligible for positions within the district. In some districts, candidates need to pass the district-level exam first before applying for any school-specific position. Only in a few districts (usually in rural Shanghai) do schools have full autonomy to hire based on a candidate's background and the school's own needs. Across those different hiring practices, however, schools generally have the opportunity to hire the teachers they need.

However, it might be helpful to conduct a school-level analysis to gain a more nuanced picture of teacher demand and supply for specific subjects. Some schools, particularly in rural districts, might have difficulty recruiting talented professionals in certain subjects. This may particularly be true for subjects that are not compulsory and are not subject to the senior secondary school or college entrance exams, such as arts, music, and physical education. In this case, the city needs to develop targeted incentives to attract more qualified candidates, such as a higher base salary or more flexible career advancement pathways.

Policy Goal 5: Leading Teachers with Strong Principals (Established)

School surveys indicate that a school principal in Shanghai has the following typical profile: a bachelor's degree (83 percent), 40–50 years old (80 percent), with an average duration in the position of 5.5 years.

Requirements for principals are stringent, and districts in Shanghai use different approaches to select principals. For example, in Jiading District, all interested individuals must obtain a principal eligibility certificate to be considered a qualified candidate. The requirements for the certificate include a written test, academic credentials, and years of service in teaching and school management. If there is an opening for a principal position, the district will select from the pool of candidates with the qualifying certificates. The district of Changning uses a different approach. Every two years, schools within the district recommend qualified teachers and administrators as candidates for the position of principal.

The group of candidates recommended by all schools form a cohort of potential contenders for positions within the district. They receive training regularly in preparation for becoming principals. This approach could potentially equip future principals with the necessary leadership and management skills, even before the job.

Research shows that rigorous in-service and leadership training and support are associated with gains in student achievement (Gates et al. 2014). Effective school principals can enhance teacher motivation and accountability. A study on schools in the United States finds that for the best principals, the rate of teacher turnover is highest in grades in which teachers are least effective (Branch, Hanushek, and Rivkin 2013). This finding supports the belief that improvement in teacher effectiveness provides an important channel through which principals can raise the quality of education (Branch, Hanushek, and Rivkin 2013).

Principals in Shanghai participate in various kinds of leadership programs based on their years of service. First-year principals face particular challenges as they make the transition into the new position. In 2013, Shanghai launched the "New Principal Training Plan" to build a strong cadre of new principals in basic education. The Shanghai Municipal Education Commission collaborated with Shanghai Normal University to develop a one-year training program, aligned with the newly released "Professional Standards for Basic Education Principals" to focus on six key topics: school planning, internal management, school culture, instructional development, teacher growth, and adjustment to the external environment. The program takes place once a week and includes group lectures, individual research projects, field visits, and mentoring by experienced principals to new principals.

Salary is linked to performance for principals in Shanghai. Principals' salaries include three components: base salary, rank-related salary, and performance-based salary. Similar to that for teachers, the performance-based salary consists of an occupation-related allowance, a workload allowance, and a performance reward. Principals can also be promoted through a progressive ranking system from fourth-grade (lowest) to first-grade and outstanding (highest). The criteria for promotion include credentials, years of services, school management, and leadership in instructional development, teaching force enhancement, and student performance. Principals are required to teach at least two classes every week to be qualified for a promotion. The rank of a principal not only carries salary implications, but also serves as an indicator of competence for further career advancement. The performance-based portion of a principal's salary is linked to overall school performance. Although districts implement their own rules related to the performance-based portion of principals' salaries, the key factor is the end-of-year district evaluation of schools.

Principals assume the role of instructional leaders in Shanghai. In 2012, the Ministry of Education released "Professional Standards for Basic Education Principals" as a key reference for capacity building and management of the principal force. The standards include six main areas, with requirements on professional skills and knowledge that principals need to possess; instructional development is identified as one key area (table 3.7).

Principals are not only expected to be familiar with students' learning targets at different stages of schooling and the related curriculum standards, but they are also considered the leader of curriculum reform and development of the school-based curriculum. The policy requires principals to observe classes regularly and provide feedback to teachers on instructional improvement. Some schools in Shanghai appoint one principal specifically in charge of instructional development. Among the 153 principals surveyed, more than two-thirds (69 percent) had observed between 31 and 50 classes during the past semester, and 15 percent had observed more than 50 classes, reflecting a consistent practice of principal class observations (table 3.8). After the observations, 99 percent of the principals

Table 3.7 Requirements for Professional Skills under "Professional Standards for Basic Education Principals"

Area	Selected requirements on professional skills
1. **School planning**	i. Lead the planning and implementation of school development plans ii. Monitor school development and make adjustments accordingly
2. **Internal management**	i. Establish school personnel and finance regulations ii. Ensure school safety and establish emergency management policies
3. **School culture**	i. Define the school education philosophy ii. Facilitate the organization of school cultural and science-related events
4. **Instructional development**	i. Execute curriculum-related guidelines and support the development and implementation of school-based curriculum ii. Observe classes and provide instructional guidance iii. Lead and organize research activities and education reform to create a comprehensive learning assessment system
5. **Teacher growth**	i. Ensure that every teacher fulfills the 360-hour professional development requirement ii. Develop professional development plans for individual teachers and provide targeted training for young teachers iii. Protect the rights of teachers and create a performance-based incentive system
6. **Adjustment to the external environment**	i. Support parent-teacher association's involvement in school operations ii. Organize events for parents to understand students' development iii. Encourage and organize teachers and students to participate in community events

Source: Shanghai Municipal Education Commission 2009 (http://www.shmec.gov.cn/web/xxgk/newsearch_do.php? pagenumber=2&searchinfo=%3A%3A%BB%A6%BD%CC%CE%AF%C8%CB%3A2009%3A%3A%3A%3A0%3A%3A&select=3).

Table 3.8 School Principals' Class Observations, School Principals Survey (N = 153)

Number of classes observed in the last semester	Number of principals observing	Percentage of principals observing
Fewer than 30	25	16
Between 31 and 40	67	44
Between 41 and 50	38	25
Between 51 and 60	14	9
More than 60	9	6

indicate that they provide feedback to the teachers, using methods such as specific discussion sessions with teachers (76 percent) and written feedback (9 percent) (table 3.9). Furthermore, principals frequently use various communication tools to interact with students, teachers, and parents. Based on the survey, 86 percent of the principals host individual meetings with students, teachers, and parents; 46 percent use online tools such as WeChat (a Chinese message application); and 61 percent have a designated letter mailbox for receiving feedback.

The principals surveyed demonstrate extensive professional knowledge. More than 95 percent of the principals have either substantial or some knowledge of students' physical and mental development stages; learning objectives and curriculum standards for main subjects; curriculum design, implementation, and evaluation; and usage of learning material (table 3.10). With regard to instruction, 99 percent of the principals have a good grasp of pedagogical theories including student learning behaviors, teachers' pedagogical role, and the knowledge construction process. However, the principals have some catching up to do in the use of information and communications technology (ICT) for learning. Even though most of the principals can use multiple media resources (81 percent) and Microsoft suites (88 percent), only 46 percent have knowledge and experience in ICT classrooms (such as distance interactive learning). About 46 percent are skilled in using electronic learning materials as a teaching resource, and only 17 percent are experienced in developing such materials.

Principals have substantial autonomy in making decisions to support teaching. Principals in most districts can hire new teachers and dismiss ineffective teachers, thus being able to make decisions beneficial to student learning outcomes (only a small number of districts use centralized teacher recruitment and distribution). In practice, however, principals rarely dismiss teachers directly. The common practice is to demote ineffective teachers to staff positions, such as lab technicians, to avoid direct conflict between the principal and the teacher.

Table 3.9 School Principals' Feedback to Teachers after Class Observation, School Principals Survey (N = 153)

Feedback mechanisms	Number of principals observing	Percentage of principals observing
No feedback, but observing the class as a criterion for teacher evaluation	1	1
Communicating with observed teacher immediately after class	9	6
Holding specific feedback discussion	117	76
Written feedback	14	9
Indirect feedback via teaching effectiveness and teacher ranking evaluation	4	3
Others	5	3
Invalid	3	2

Table 3.10 School Principals' Professional Knowledge in Shanghai, School Principals Survey (N = 153)

percent

Knowledge area	Very familiar	Familiar	Not very familiar	Unfamiliar
Students' physical and mental development stages	80	20	0	0
Learning objectives of main subjects	49	47	3	0
Curriculum criteria of main subjects	45	51	3	1
Curriculum design, implementation, and evaluation	63	36	1	0
Usage of learning material	79	20	1	0
Usage of multiple media	32	49	16	2
Production of teaching materials (for example, PowerPoint presentations)	41	47	10	1
Usage of information and communications technology (for example, distance interactive instruction)	14	46	36	3
Usage of electronic material	12	34	39	16
Development of electronic teaching material	4	13	42	41
Construction of school curriculum system based on information and communications technology	5	25	40	30

Principals also have the authority to determine the performance-based portion of teacher salaries to reward strong performers. With those levers, principals play a key role in pedagogy support and teacher management.

Policy Goal 6: Monitoring Teaching and Learning (Advanced)

Adequate data on student learning outcomes are available to inform teaching and policy. Assessments in Shanghai follow a multilevel model. At the school level, students participate in weekly or biweekly subject quizzes to demonstrate their progress in each learning unit. Schools administer midterm and final examinations for key subjects (Chinese, math, English, plus physics and chemistry in secondary school) every semester to evaluate overall student outcomes. As the designers and graders of the assessments, teachers have complete information about students' scores. School homework is regularly assigned and feedback provided. The results of the assessments inform their teaching practices—for example, they can rearrange lesson plans to repeat certain concepts and theories. Teachers can also use the results to tailor after-class help sessions for individual students. The average score on midterm and final examinations for every class is often available to all teachers teaching the same subject in the same grade.

The availability of data serves a diagnostic purpose: it encourages teachers to identify areas for improvement in instructional practice; it also allows the school to analyze the strengths and weaknesses of teachers to target professional development activities.

Shanghai administers citywide examinations at the end of the compulsory nine-year education period. At the end of ninth grade, students take the written senior secondary school entrance examination in the subjects of Chinese, math, English, physics, and chemistry. Physical education, lab operations, and the moral ethics of students also factor into their final examination scores. The total score on the examination determines the type of senior secondary school in which students will enroll: admission into highly selective model senior secondary schools requires outstanding performance on the examination. Roughly half of the students who do not achieve good results will enroll in technical and vocational schools while the other better-performing half generally enrolls in general and model senior secondary schools. At the end of twelfth grade, students take a nationwide college entrance exam (*gao kao*), the score of which determines whether and in which type of university the student will be able to enroll.

Leaders at the district level and the school level have full access to the data on student outcomes. Districts use the data to evaluate overall school performance, while schools use the data to assess the effectiveness of individual teachers.

Shanghai has been a pioneer in participating in international assessments in China. The city was the top performer in the PISA in both 2009 and 2012. Results on PISA have been used for country-level comparisons.

Teacher performance is monitored through multiple mechanisms. All schools in Shanghai regularly monitor teacher performance. Under the 2012 State Council's "Advice on Strengthening the Teaching Force," schools are encouraged to carry out a comprehensive teacher monitoring and evaluation process that does not solely focus on student test results. The assessment should also take into consideration teachers' moral ethics, competence, and contribution to the school. The school principal and senior teachers conduct classroom observations to monitor teacher performance. In addition, districts organize regular supervision of teaching at each school. The capacity of the teaching force is a core indicator in district-level school evaluations. Furthermore, all workers in China, teachers included, have a personnel file that tracks work-related ranks, rewards, and punishments. If a teacher decides to transfer, the personnel file will be reviewed by the receiving school. In practice, 90 percent of the schools surveyed also create an individual professional development profile for each teacher, which often includes the teacher's development goals, the name and type of research papers published, the teacher's training experience, and his or her achievements such as awards and titles. Therefore, a system is in place to track teacher performance over time.

Teacher performance is evaluated using various sources. At the school level, the principal conducts annual teacher performance evaluations with the involvement of other senior administrators or senior teachers. The evaluation encompasses multiple dimensions: a self-evaluation of strengths and weaknesses, classroom observations of teaching practices, student performance, participation in research activities, and interaction with students are all taken into consideration. The comprehensive assessment allows principals to gain a clear understanding of where each teacher stands and offers a mechanism through which principals can provide teachers with yearly feedback to improve performance.

Policy Goal 7: Supporting Teachers to Improve Instruction (Established)

Professional development is an essential part of teacher responsibilities. In Shanghai, all new basic education teachers are required to complete 360 hours of professional development during the first five years of their teaching careers, which is equivalent to nine days every year. If a teacher wants to apply for a senior-grade rank, he or she must complete another 540 hours of training, equivalent to 67.5 days. Not only do teachers receive most of the training free of charge, but they are also reimbursed for their transportation and accommodation expenses. This training requirement provides a base guarantee that every teacher receives appropriate development opportunities and professional support, especially when they first enter the profession. According to the school survey results, on average, schools spend 7 percent of their total operational expenditures on teachers' professional development. In addition, 92 percent have set up specific policies on teacher training; 71 percent have created policies evaluating teachers' professional development; and 73 percent have created policies providing teachers with incentives to undertake professional development.

A series of experimental studies has found that professional development activities of less than 14 hours appear to have no effect on teachers' effectiveness. Meanwhile, learning opportunities averaging about 50 hours over a period of 6 to 12 months, with well-designed and content-specific materials, were associated with gains of up to 21 percentile points on the achievement tests used to evaluate student learning (Darling-Hammond, Wei, and Andree 2010). Shanghai meets this critical requirement quite well. However, the required duration of professional development in Shanghai is slightly lower than that in neighboring high-performing countries like Japan, Korea, and Singapore (figure 3.7).

Additionally, much of the professional development is designed to be school-based and collaborative and to pay particular attention to instructional improvement. Basic education in Shanghai has a long history of establishing professional communities to improve teachers' instructional competencies. Among the multiple professional development options, two practices merit particular attention: teaching-research groups (box 3.4) and lesson observations (box 3.5). These activities expose teachers to best instructional practices and leverage every teacher's knowledge and skills to contribute to the improvement of the collective teaching community.

Figure 3.7 Officially Required Days of Professional Training per Year, Secondary Education

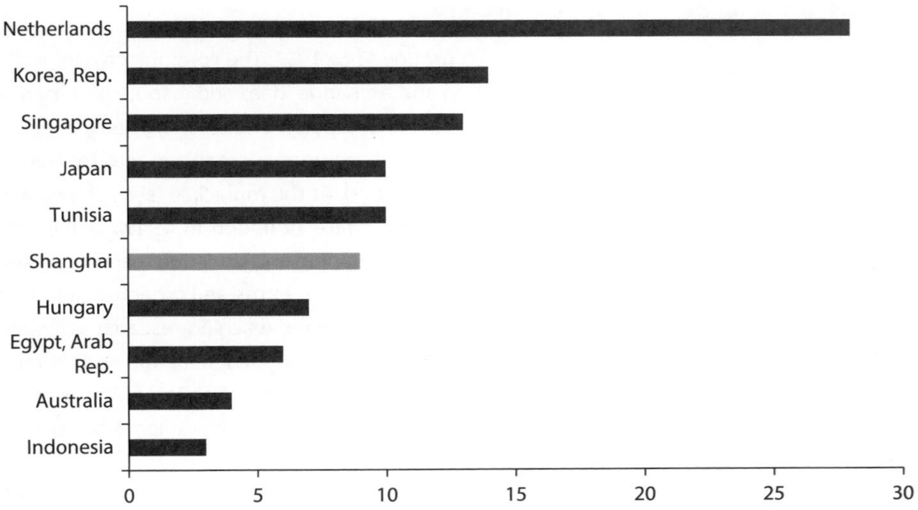

Sources: Data from OECD 2009; World Bank 2011.

A similar model is in effect in Japan, the Lesson Study Approach, which is an interesting example of a simple and sustainable in-service training model (see box 3.6). Job-embedded teacher-to-teacher support and in-service training provide contextually relevant professional development opportunities to teachers.

In addition to the teaching-research groups and lesson observations, at the city level Shanghai provides tiered professional development that targets teachers with different backgrounds. For novice teachers, Shanghai uses the one-year in-service induction program as mentioned above. For teachers with a number of years of experience, Shanghai launched a program in 2014 to encourage group collaboration for conducting research and developing curriculum. In the program's first year, 32 groups were awarded a total of RMB 300,000 as financial support for their three-year projects. For experienced teachers, the city aims to develop among them a team of research talent with "dual skills"—teaching and management skills for leading the teaching field. A number of experienced teachers and principals have received training to further hone their pedagogical and management skills. Under the dual-skills training, 3,000 principals and teachers have benefited and 70 have been appointed principals of Shanghai's model schools.

Teachers' professional development is aligned with perceived needs. The "Municipal Primary and Secondary School Curriculum Plan" stipulates that school leaders should create targeted teacher training plans based on the results of each teacher's evaluation. New teachers are assigned mentors to help strengthen their performance. If a teacher receives an unsatisfactory result in an evaluation, he or she is paired with a supervisor or senior teacher to receive monitoring and help. Clear and explicit standards for teaching and learning provide another link between teacher professional development and perceived needs.

Box 3.4 Teaching-Research Groups in China

China has been promoting teaching-research groups since 1957. The core objective of such groups is to allow teachers to conduct research and exchange ideas and resources on pedagogy and curriculum so as to improve their instructional capacity and teaching quality.

The structure of these teaching-research groups is commonly organized into four tiers: national, provincial or municipal, district, and school level. At the municipal level, Shanghai's Municipal Education Commission Teaching-Research Office (founded in 1949), is the key agency responsible for designing curriculum plans, developing and updating teaching material, conducting analysis of basic education quality, proposing reforms, and organizing teacher training. In particular, the office organizes city-level systematic teaching-research activities and collects best teaching practices from districts and schools for dissemination and promotion. Each district in Shanghai also hosts a Teaching-Research Office. The Teaching-Research Office at the district level is often housed in the district's Teacher Training Colleges or Centers, which have a mandate for in-service teacher training.

At the school level, teaching-research groups function as a professional development platform consisting of teachers of the same subject. In larger schools, the groups are often further divided by grade. Each group has a leader who is responsible for organizing the activities and introducing novice teachers to the active learning community. The leader is also held accountable for overall teacher development in the group. The groups normally meet for two to three hours every week. In every teaching-research group, the major activities include

- Teacher professional development
- Coaching and guidance by senior teachers for junior teachers
- Induction of new teachers (almost 99 percent of surveyed schools have induction programs)
- Research on new subject content and pedagogical practices (84 percent of surveyed schools have established an overarching research topic for all teachers, 81 percent encourage individual-topic research, and 88 percent provide research topic options for teachers)
- Teacher performance evaluation by teachers within the same group, based on the frequency, intensity, and achievements in the group activities.

The collaborative nature of teaching-research groups allows for the growth of the entire teaching community, rather than a few individuals. The tiered network of teaching-research groups at the municipal, district, and school levels enables quick and far-reaching dissemination of curriculum best practices.

In practice, teaching-research groups are a core aspect of teacher activities: 99 percent of the 153 schools surveyed host Teaching-Research Groups for different subjects and 100 percent have specific requirements on teaching-research activities; 44 percent host teaching-research group activities once a week and 53 percent host the activities once every two weeks. Some 85 percent of schools provide funding for the groups while 100 percent encourage teachers to participate in research projects. In addition, 92 percent of the principals surveyed consider school-level activities to be highly important for teachers' professional development, 29 percent put high importance on the Municipal Teaching-Research Office, and 59 percent consider the district-level Teaching-Research Office highly important.

Box 3.5 Lesson Observations, Shanghai

Lesson observations take place throughout a teacher's career in Shanghai. Within the school, junior teachers engage in regular lesson observations of senior teachers to learn best practices. Reciprocally, senior teachers observe junior teachers' lessons to provide feedback. Sometimes teachers teaching the same subject observe each other's practices to provide peer feedback. This model allows teachers to benefit from one another's experience and serves as a supportive mechanism to bring new or struggling teachers to the level of their peers. There are lesson competitions (*gong kai ke*) at the school, district, and city levels. Teachers prepare a lesson and showcase it to the school community or a larger audience at the district or city level. Those with the best instructional practices are rewarded and the lesson is shared with the teaching community at large. Participation in those lesson competitions is also an important factor in teacher evaluations.

Tennessee has imported the model of lesson observations in its pilot Teacher Peer Excellence Group (TPEG). A group of 18 school principals traveled to China in 2013 to learn the practice. Upon their return, TPEG was rolled out in a number of schools in the state. Under TPEG, a group of teachers engage in collaborative lesson planning and peer lesson observations. Actionable, specific feedback is provided by the team to further refine the teaching practice. Preliminary research on this program shows encouraging results in teacher evaluations (Cheshier 2015).

Box 3.6 Japan's Lesson Study Approach

In Japan *kenkyuu jugyou* (research lessons) are a key part of the learning culture. Every teacher periodically prepares a best possible lesson that demonstrates strategies for achieving a specific goal (for example, students becoming active problem-solvers or students learning more from each other) in collaboration with other colleagues. A group of teachers observes while the lesson is taught and the lesson is usually recorded in a number of ways, including videotape, audiotape, and narrative or checklist observations that focus on areas of interest to the instructing teacher (for example, how many students volunteered their own ideas). Afterward, the group of teachers, and sometimes outside educators, discuss the lesson's strengths and weakness, ask questions, and make suggestions for improving the lesson. In some cases the revised lesson is given by another teacher a few days later and observed and discussed again.

Teachers themselves determine the theme and frequency of research lessons. Large study groups often break up into subgroups of four to six teachers. The subgroups plan their own lessons but work toward the same goal, and teachers from all subgroups share and comment on lessons and try to attend the lesson and follow-up discussion. For a typical lesson study, the 10–15 hours of group meetings are spread over three to four weeks. While schools let out between 2:40 and 3:45 p.m., teachers' work days do not end until 5 p.m., which provides additional time for collegial work and planning. Most lesson study meetings occur during the

box continues next page

Box 3.6 Japan's Lesson Study Approach *(continued)*

hours after school lets out. The research lessons allow teachers to refine individual lessons, consult with other teachers and get colleagues' observations about their classroom practice, reflect on their own practice, learn new content and approaches, and build a culture that emphasizes continuous improvement and collaboration. Some teachers also give public research lessons, which expedites the spread of best practices across schools; allows principals, district personnel, and policy makers to see how teachers are grappling with new subject matter and goals; and gives recognition to excellent teachers.

Source: Darling-Hammond, Wei, and Andree 2010, 4.

Policy Goal 8: Motivating Teachers to Perform (Established)

Opportunities for promotion are linked to performance. As mentioned, the performance of teachers that seek promotion to a higher rank must be evaluated. All new teachers in Shanghai have a one-year probationary period. At the end of their first year, teachers who do not pass the annual evaluation are not granted a contract to continue teaching. This screening mechanism ensures that all new teachers are qualified to continue teaching.

Accountability mechanisms are in place for teachers. According to State Council's "Advice on Strengthening the Teaching Force," teachers need to complete 360 hours of professional development during their first five years of teaching to assist in the transition to the teaching career and ensure that teachers have a baseline level of knowledge and skills. Furthermore, principals at every school conduct annual teacher performance evaluations to identify strong teachers as instructional leaders and assist weak teachers with improvement. Of the schools surveyed, 98 percent have written documentation of their evaluation systems for both teachers and students. The "Guidelines for Regular Accreditation of Primary and Secondary Teachers (Tentative)" require teachers to be accredited once every five years to continue teaching. Requirements include passing the teacher performance evaluation and fulfilling 360 hours of professional development. According to the Teachers Law, teachers can be dismissed for misconduct, child abuse, and poor performance.

In addition to these explicit mechanisms, there is a strong sense of professional accountability among teachers and principals in Shanghai. As put by one teacher in Shanghai,

> Teachers always have the option of spending 10–15 minutes to review the homework and previous day work with the students so that challenging knowledge points where students make the most mistakes can be further elucidated. These 10–15 minute periods make a world of difference in enhancing student grasp of the knowledge points. Most of teachers in Shanghai routinely do this. (Personal interview with Mr. Xia, a veteran teacher, and current dean of education department, Shanghai Normal University, 2015.)

Some compensation is linked to performance. In a teacher's monthly salary, the performance-based proportion is allocated based on the overall results from the teacher evaluation. Another performance-based incentive is based on the teacher ranking framework. High-performing teachers can apply for higher teacher ranks, which entail a higher base salary. Since the implementation of performance pay in 2009 (through the Ministry of Education statement "Guidance about Performance Based Pay in Compulsory Education"), the impact of these mechanisms has been evaluated. The main positive impacts include (1) reducing the teacher pay disparity between districts, as teachers in the remote rural districts tend to benefit most from performance pay; (2) contributing to the balanced development of core versus noncore subjects given that teaching hours are directly linked with pay so noncore teachers have equal incentive to teach the noncore subjects as the core subjects; (3) further motivating teachers to engage in professional development because a portion of pay is based on a performance evaluation.

However, a few challenges have emerged with regard to the design and implementation of the performance schemes. First, the magnitude of the performance pay may not be significant enough, especially for a few central districts that already have a higher base pay for teachers. Second, because the scheme is also based on years of experience, academic qualifications, and workload, the pay of those teachers who do not reach the established minimum standards will actually be lower than before the scheme. Finally, the performance pay scheme consolidated several fragmented subsidy and in-kind benefit schemes, and as a result, some teachers felt that their overall level of pay and benefits may have decreased.

Much controversy surrounded the performance pay scheme when it was initially implemented. Going forward, it is important to continue research into the impact of the scheme to determine how teachers respond to the incentives. Understanding teachers' attitudes toward specific incentive programs is crucial to the success and effectiveness of this policy (OECD 2011b). It is also important to review the administrative processes through which incentives are introduced because procedural complications could be detrimental to the original intent of the policy itself (Lewis and Springer 2008).

Summary

The use of SABER–Teachers questionnaires to assess teacher-related policies and practices in Shanghai yields a comprehensive picture of the way in which teachers are selected, developed, supported, and evaluated. Based on the rubrics, this exercise finds that Shanghai scores at least "established" in all eight policy goals related to teachers, including (1) setting clear expectations for teachers, (2) attracting the best into teaching, (3) preparing teachers with useful training and experience, (4) matching teachers' skills with students' needs, (5) leading teachers with strong principals, (6) monitoring teaching and learning, (7) supporting teachers to improve instruction, and (8) motivating teachers to perform.

Figure 3.8 summarizes the essence of teacher development policies in Shanghai. A three-pillar teacher development system effectively promotes teaching excellence in Shanghai. Teachers are provided with a career ladder, supported with elaborate school-based professional development and in-service training through teaching-research groups, and their performance is evaluated accordingly and linked to career progression and performance pay. This comprehensive professional development framework incorporates multiple layers of in-service training, evaluation of teacher performance, and a structured career ladder that provides both motivation and a mechanism for teachers to progress in their careers, which is key to Shanghai's demonstrated excellence in education.

The benchmarking and implementation survey also points to a number of areas in which Shanghai can focus its future reform efforts on teachers. Areas such as teacher distribution and the implementation and impact of performance pay based on the teacher career ladder were not explicitly assessed but turn out to be important dimensions.

First, *the teacher recruitment entry criteria* should be upgraded to require at least a bachelor's degree. This practice will bring Shanghai up to the level of most of the OECD and other developed Asian countries. In reality, most of the applicants already have a bachelor's degree. The explicit recognition of the higher requirement will reduce unnecessary inefficiency in the recruitment process. Moreover, it will send a positive signal for the teaching profession.

Figure 3.8 Shanghai's Teacher Development Framework

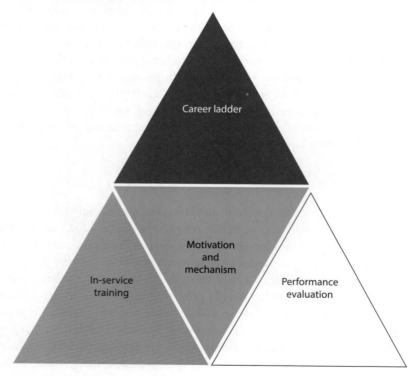

Source: Adapted from Zhang, Ding, and Xu 2016.

Additionally, Shanghai could increase the explicit number of professional development days. The formal, course-based professional development requirement in Shanghai (9 days) is slightly lower than in neighboring high-performing countries like Japan (10 days), Singapore (13 days), and Korea (14 days). On the other hand, Shanghai clearly stands out in its multiple layers of teacher professional development, with particular emphasis on school-based activities and teacher research groups.

Another area for improvement is the *equitable distribution of teachers*, especially qualified and experienced teachers, between rural and urban districts, and between model schools and regular schools. SABER does not fully address this issue and further analysis of the matter is warranted. Sufficient related research seems to indicate that more qualified and experienced teachers tend to concentrate in high-performing and urban districts. Furthermore, anecdotal evidence shows that rural and low-performing school districts are more likely to be understaffed in nontesting subjects such as arts, music, and physical education. Another shortage area may be in special education. As Shanghai moves toward mainstreaming special education students into regular classrooms, teachers trained in special education will be in higher demand. It would be helpful to conduct a more detailed school-level analysis in the future to gain a more nuanced picture of teacher distribution and demand and supply for specific subjects.

Finally, very little research is available concerning the implementation and impact of the current *teacher career ladder and performance pay system*. Much anecdotal evidence suggests that promotion of teachers within the professional ladder and the distribution of performance pay may in practice be overly tied to research and publication, to the extent that some teachers are forced to forge research data and purchase publications just to satisfy the requirements for promotion. There have also been reports that the criteria may not be entirely transparent.

References

Boyd, D., P. Grossman, H. Lankford, S. Loeb, and J. Wyckoff. 2006. "How Changes in Entry Requirements Alter the Teacher Workforce and Affect Student Achievement." *Education Finance and Policy* 1 (2): 176–216.

Branch, G. F., E. Hanushek, and S. G. Rivkin. 2013. "School Leaders Matter." *Education Next* 13 (1): 62–69. http://hanushek.stanford.edu/sites/default/files/publications/Branch%2BHanushek%2BRivkin%202013%20EdNext%2013%281%29_0.pdf.

Cheshier, T. 2015. "From Shanghai to Collierville, Collaboration Model Boosts Teacher Performance." Chalkbeat Tennessee website. http://tn.chalkbeat.org/2015/01/28/from-shanghai-to-collierville-collaboration-model-boosts-teacher-performance/#.Vj3iL_krLIU.

China Statistical Yearbook. 2015. "Average Wage of Employed Persons in Urban Units by Sector." http://www.stats.gov.cn/tjsj/ndsj/2015/html/EN0415.jpg.

Darling-Hammond, L., R. C. Wei, and A. Andree. 2010. "How High-Achieving Countries Develop Great Teachers." Stanford Center for Opportunity Policy in Education, Stanford University, Stanford, CA. https://edpolicy.stanford.edu/publications/pubs/291.

Dolton, P. J. 1990. "The Economics of UK Teacher Supply: The Graduate's Decision." *Economic Journal* 100: 91–104.

Education Bureau of Jiading District of Shanghai. 2014. "Shang Hai Shi Jia Ding Qu Shen Hua Zhong Xiao Xue Jiao Shi Zhi Cheng Gai Ge Fang An." http://wenku.baidu.com /link?url=SSB8AhCM9Y_eEBpfA9k7SZJF7a7nbqoe5fvENOfvoJ7P4YX5UVdw 9nUyBOhC9lsWbIs75NDusjrLvSE_U3rHjTuJa2-hrmap-b2OyRjesmG.

Gates, Susan M., Laura S. Hamilton, Paco Martorell, Susan Burkhauser, Paul Heaton, Ashley Pierson, Matthew Baird, Mirka Vuollo, Jennifer J. Li, Diana Lavery, Melody Harvey, and Kun Gu. 2014. "Principal Preparation Matters: How Leadership Affects Student Achievement." RAND Corporation, Santa Monica, CA. http://www.rand.org /pubs/research_briefs/RB9786.

Lewis, J., and M. Springer. 2008. "Performance Incentives in Texas: Why Schools Chose Not to Participate." Performance Brief, National Center on Performance Incentives, Nashville, TN. https://my.vanderbilt.edu/performanceincentives/files/2012/10/Lewis _and_Springer_for_posting.pdf.

OECD (Organisation for Economic Co-operation and Development). 2009. *Creating Effective Teaching and Learning Environments: First Results from TALIS.* Paris: OECD Publishing.

———. 2011a. *Education at a Glance 2011: OECD Indicators.* Paris: OECD Publishing.

———. 2011b. *Evaluating and Rewarding the Quality of Teachers: International Practices.* Paris: OECD Publishing.

———. 2013. "Teaching and Learning International Survey (TALIS); Complete Database 2013." OECD, Paris. http://stats.oecd.org/Index.aspx?datasetcode=talis_2013%20.

———. 2014. "Shanghai (China) – Country note: Results from TALIS 2013-14." OECD, Paris. http://www.oecd.org/edu/school/TALIS-2014-country-note-Shanghai.pdf

Shan, Z. 2013. *China Teacher Development Report 2012.* Education Science Press.

Shanghai Municipal Education Commission. 2005. "Curriculum Standards for Primary and Secondary Schools in Shanghai." http://www.shmec.gov.cn/web/hdpt/wsgs _detail.php?subject_id=48#go_top.

Wolter, S. C., and S. Denzler. 2003. "Wage Elasticity of the Teacher Supply in Switzerland." Discussion Paper 733, Institute for the Study of Labor, Bonn.

World Bank. 2011. "Tunisia Teacher Policy: SABER Country Report." World Bank, Washington, DC. http://wbgfiles.worldbank.org/documents/hdn/ed/saber/supporting _doc/CountryReports/TCH/SABER_Teachers_Tunisia_CR_Final_2011.pdf.

———. 2013. "What Matters Most for Teacher Policies: A Framework Paper." SABER Working Paper 4, World Bank, Washington, DC. http://wbgfiles.worldbank.org /documents/hdn/ed/saber/supporting_doc/Background/TCH/Framework_SABER -Teachers.pdf.

———. 2016. "Pupil-Teacher Ratio in Primary Education." World Bank, Washington, DC. http://data.worldbank.org/indicator/SE.PRM.ENRL.TC.ZS.

Xu, B. 2014. Modern Primary and Secondary Education Journal. Northeast Normal University, Changchun, Jilin, China.

Zhang, M., X. Ding, and J. Xu. 2016. "Developing Shanghai's Teachers: Teacher Quality Systems in Top Performing Countries." The National Center on Education and Economy, Washington, DC.

CHAPTER 4

Financing Education for Quality and Equity

Introduction

The Finance module of the Systems Approach for Better Education Results (SABER–Finance) takes stock of five aspects of school finance policies: (1) school conditions and resources, (2) allocation mechanisms, (3) revenue sources, (4) education spending, and (5) fiscal control and capacity. Data gathered through surveys with 153 principals, key informant interviews with teachers and officials of the Shanghai Municipal Education Commission, and review of local and global policy and research literature are used to complement the SABER policy instruments to shed light on the extent to which policies are implemented.

SABER–Finance analyzes the collected data to assess whether the education finance system effectively realizes six policy goals: (1) ensuring basic conditions for learning, (2) monitoring learning conditions and outcomes, (3) overseeing service delivery, (4) budgeting with adequate and transparent information, (5) providing more resources to students who need them, and (6) managing resources efficiently (see figure 4.1). This instrument also provides a holistic review of whether each education finance system is making progress in achieving adequacy, equity, and efficiency. The scope of the analysis is limited primarily to public schools.

Overall, it has been ascertained on the basis of SABER–Finance that Shanghai's policy environment for educational finance can be scored between "established" and "advanced" (table 4.1).

Policy Goal 1: Ensuring Basic Conditions for Learning (Advanced)

Detailed policies are in place ensuring basic educational inputs of infrastructure, learning materials, and teachers. Specific regulations stipulate the basic requirements for school infrastructure inputs such as safety and environmental construction standards, square footage per student, drinking water, hygienic facilities, and electricity in Shanghai. In addition to physical infrastructure, learning materials

Figure 4.1 Six Policy Goals under SABER–Finance

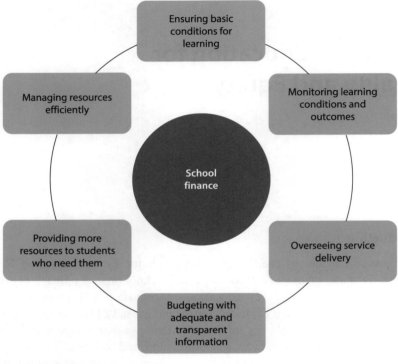

Source: Vegas and Coffin 2013.
Note: SABER = Systems Approach for Better Education Results.

are readily available for students. As of 2007, schools are required to provide free textbooks to students. The municipal textbook supervision committee annually produces a catalog of approved textbooks for schools to select and order from designated local bookstores. The national government has also released guidelines for schools to improve the conditions of their libraries and computer labs to aid learning. The provision of infrastructure and learning materials can contribute to student learning by enabling an environment conducive to learning for students and adequate working conditions for teachers.

With regard to teacher qualifications, primary school teachers are required to have at least a three-year tertiary vocational college degree (equivalent to the International Standard Classification of Education [ISCED] 5B level) and secondary teachers need to have at least a four-year bachelor's degree (equivalent to the ISCED 5A level). However, in practice, more than 97 percent of current teachers in Shanghai already possess bachelor's degrees (table 4.2). Only 1.3 percent of teachers have three-year vocational degrees. As mentioned in chapter 3, this educational requirement can be strengthened to be equivalent to requirements for basic education teachers in other high-performing countries, who often have a bachelor's degree equivalent to ISCED 5A.

Table 4.1 SABER–Finance Scoring, Shanghai

Policy and resource framework (Goals and levers)	SABER score
Ensuring basic conditions for learning	●●●●
1. Setting policies to ensure basic inputs	●●●○
2. Establishing learning goals	●●●●
Monitoring learning conditions and outcomes	●●●○
1. Setting systems to monitor learning conditions	●●●○
2. Setting systems to assess learning outcomes	●●●●
Overseeing service delivery	●●●○
1. Setting mechanisms to verify availability of physical resources at schools	●●●○
2. Setting mechanisms to verify availability of human resources at schools	●●●○
Budgeting with adequate and transparent information	●●●○
1. Setting an informed budgeting process	●●●○
2. Ensuring comprehensiveness and transparency of the budgeting process	●●●●
Providing more resources to students in need	●●●○
1. Providing public resources to students from disadvantaged backgrounds	●●○○[a]
2. Setting school fees to represent a share of income for low-income families	●●●●
Managing resources efficiently	●●●●
1. Setting systems to verify the efficient use of educational resources	●●●●
2. Ensuring regular audits of education expenditures	●●●●

Note: Scoring rubric: Latent (●○○○), Emerging (●●○○), Established (●●●○), Advanced (●●●●).
SABER = Systems Approach for Better Education Results.
a. In consultation with the SABER–Teacher team; the reason behind the score of "emerging" was the fact that Shanghai's "disadvantaged" students need to update their status on a yearly basis.

Table 4.2 Actual Qualifications of New Teachers in Junior Secondary Schools in Shanghai
percent

Minimum requirement	Overall	Public	Private	Urban	Rural
Three-year tertiary vocational college	1.3	1	3	0	4
Four-year bachelor's degree	97.4	98	95	99	96
Master's degree	1.3	1	1	1	0

Shanghai has also established guidelines for staffing norms in basic education to ensure a sufficient number of teachers are available. Each class should have no more than 40 students. The student-to-teacher ratio should be approximately 21:1 in urban districts and 18:1 in rural districts. In secondary education, the ratio should be approximately 18:1.

However, in practice, disparities between schools still exist in the level of basic inputs. The 2015 National Compulsory Education Quality Monitoring Assessment revealed that in general public schools are better endowed than private schools in Shanghai and urban schools do better than rural schools (table 4.3).

Urban and central districts in Shanghai tend to have more generous teacher-to-student ratios and attract more highly qualified teachers compared

Table 4.3 School Resources by Type of School in Shanghai
ratio (standard deviation)

	Proportion of qualified teachers	Condition of teacher shortage	Class size	Richness of extracurricular activities	Student-to-teacher ratio	Quality of physical infrastructure	Quality of educational resources
Public	0.94 (0.18)	0.93 (2.86)	38 (22)	1.91 (2.25)	10.11 (9.65)	−0.36 (2.54)	0.02 (2.82)
Private	0.84 (0.26)	1.03 (3.25)	41 (16)	2.5 (1.45)	15.21 (12.08)	−0.48 (3.49)	−0.17 (3.95)
Overall	0.94 (0.2)	0.94 (2.88)	39 (21)	1.96 (2.22)	10.55 (10.38)	−0.37 (2.63)	0.01 (2.93)

Source: Data from OECD 2012.
Note: Standard deviation in parentheses.

Figure 4.2 Cross-District Differences in Teacher-to-Student Ratios in Shanghai Primary and Junior Secondary Schools

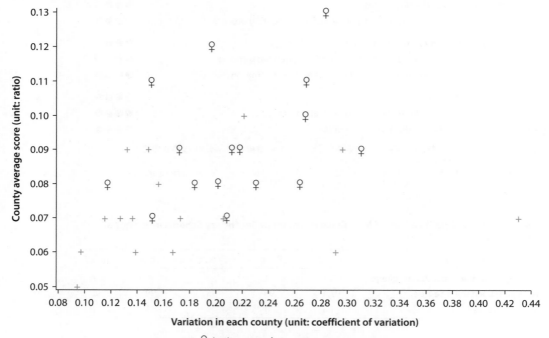

Source: Data from Ministry of Education of China 2014.

with suburban and rural districts (figures 4.2 and 4.3). The disparities can be mainly attributed to the cumulative results of the uneven fiscal capabilities of the districts. The same national monitoring report also confirms that Shanghai has the least disparity in the level of inputs compared with other provinces of China.

Learning goals have been established in Shanghai's education system with regard to completion, progression, and knowledge and skills. The city has established a set of completion and progress goals for basic education. For primary education, the target enrollment rate is 100 percent and target graduation rate is

Figure 4.3 Cross-District Differences in Proportion of Teachers with Higher-than-Required Certificate in Shanghai Primary and Junior Secondary Schools

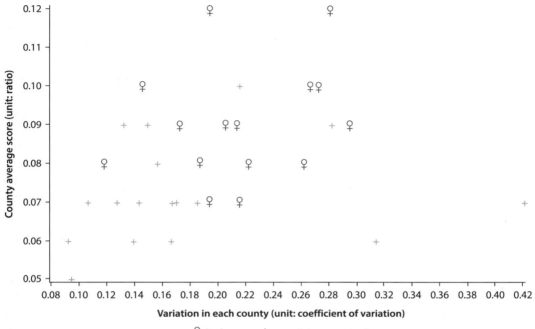

Source: Data from Ministry of Education of China 2014.

99 percent or higher. For secondary education, the graduation rate goal is 90 percent or higher. The city's basic education system also has to fulfill goals for grade repetition (less than 1 percent for primary education and less than 2 percent for secondary education) and a 0 percent dropout rate. In addition, more than 95 percent of students need to pass a physical education exam and more than 80 percent of students are expected to participate in extracurricular activities in arts and science. These specific learning goals would allow the education finance system to more effectively channel resources to inputs that contribute to quality education. Shanghai has made significant strides in basic education performance. In 2014, the city's student progression rate to senior secondary school reached 97 percent.

Shanghai's education system sets learning objectives on the knowledge areas and skills students need to master as they progress through basic education, as specified in the curriculum standards for each subject. Schools administer midterm and final examinations to assess students' progress in achieving these learning objectives. In addition, the city administers graduation examinations at the end of fifth grade and ninth grade to assess citywide student learning outcomes. The learning objectives enable teachers to align their daily work with students' learning. They also allow the school finance system to measure success in achieving quality education.

Policy Goal 2: Monitoring Learning Conditions and Outcomes (Established)

Learning conditions in schools are closely monitored. The city collects information on many aspects of schools, including drinking water, hygienic facilities, electricity, libraries, laboratories, and qualified teachers. Districts in Shanghai also conduct regular school inspections to verify whether policies on learning conditions are strictly implemented. This close monitoring ensures that schools are held accountable for providing basic educational inputs. In addition, the school census is produced annually to provide up-to-date data on student enrollment and teacher information at the school level. Each district collects the data from its schools and submits it to the city for data compilation at the municipal level once every year (enrollment data are submitted once every semester) through an electronic system. Some schools also collect more detailed information from students, such as family background, for the schools' own use in developing tailored education strategies. However, Shanghai has some catching up to do in its use of information technology in school data collection. Although 95 percent of the schools indicate that their student registration profiles (with basic student background information) are completely or mostly in an electronic format, only 72 percent keep student growth profiles (with more detailed information on student achievement over the years) and 67 percent keep teacher professional development profiles completely or mostly in an electronic format.

The Asian region contains some of the world's most advanced information-driven societies, as well as some that are at the very early stages of development. Among the most developed countries with information policies are China, Japan, the Republic of Korea, and Singapore. Japan is moving toward achieving total and easy access to information driven by the u-Japan Policy Package.[1] Singapore's e-Gov[2] and Korea's "Informatization" policies[3] strive for complete coverage. The availability of information on students, teachers, and infrastructure in an electronic format allows policy makers to retrieve information promptly and monitor trends and changes in learning conditions to make timely adjustments in resource allocations. In an effort to enhance the collection of data on education and its subsequent analysis, Shanghai is building a comprehensive education management information system (EMIS) that integrates basic education statistics such as enrollment and teacher attendance and more detailed student learning outcomes. This EMIS can be an effective tool for tracking student growth and conducting specific analyses of student learning. It is, however, important to study how improved access to education information and data on competency and satisfaction levels of students, teachers, and parents as well as groups most directly affected by education policies is being analyzed and used. Additionally, how are the level of electronic data collection and the resources being allocated to the process being measured? What is the rate of achievement across various groups? Efforts need to be made to better understand the relationship between improving access to data and achievement to effectively reform and use the present EMIS in Shanghai.

City and nationwide student exams are administered annually to measure student learning outcomes. In addition to monitoring school inputs, a high-quality education system collects regular information on student learning outcomes. As mentioned in SABER–Teachers (chapter 3), all students take the city-level graduation examination (*zhong kao*) at the end of ninth grade. This exam also serves as the selection test for senior secondary school, making it a high-stakes test as well. Scores from the test determine whether students will progress to senior secondary school and which type of senior secondary school they will enter. At the end of the senior secondary level (twelfth grade), students take a college entrance examination (*gao kao*) that determines whether and where a student will go to college.[4] The data from these assessments help policy makers track progress on curriculum standards and trends in student learning outcomes. Policy makers also have access to the assessment data disaggregated by district and by school, and each school has student-specific performance scores.

School Evaluations

Although the city sets targets for completion and progression to encourage overall achievement, and data can be disaggregated by school, schools are not evaluated based on their students' scores or rate of enrollment in senior secondary schools. Because the student population profile differs substantially across schools, this policy discourages schools from being heavily score driven and does not penalize schools that host a large number of academically challenged or disadvantaged students. Two types of school evaluations are conducted in Shanghai:

1. Regular school supervision is conducted by each district's education supervision office. According to the national "Regulations for Education Supervision" and Shanghai's "Advice on Promoting School Developmental Supervision and Evaluation (tentative)," the district's education supervision office visits district schools at least once a year. The comprehensive supervision uses each school's development plan as an important reference point and encompasses pedagogical, operational, and personnel aspects.

2. Shanghai has also been implementing a comprehensive school evaluation system that goes beyond student achievement assessments—the "Green Indicators of Academic Quality of Primary and Secondary School Students"—since 2011. The instrument comprises questionnaires for students, teachers, and principals. It aims to assess school quality in a holistic fashion, including students' motivation for learning, academic burden, and student-teacher relationships (see table 4.4). Every year, the city selects a random sample of schools in basic education across districts for the assessment. In 2011, 804 schools/principals along with 63,640 students (fourth graders and ninth graders) and 9,445 teachers participated. The students took academic performance assessments, filled out surveys, and were tested for physical health. The teachers and principals completed a survey. The city uses the results to evaluate the overall academic quality of basic education and reveal gaps for improvement.

Table 4.4 Green Indicators of Academic Quality of Primary and Secondary School Students

1. Student's academic performance
2. Student's learning motivation
3. Student's academic burden
4. Student-teacher relationship
5. Teacher pedagogy
6. Principal's leadership in curriculum development
7. Effect of student's socioeconomic background on achievement
8. Student's moral behavior
9. Student's physical and mental health
10. Progress on Indicators 1–9

Source: Shanghai Municipal Education Commission 2011.

In addition to an annual municipal report on the assessment results, the city produces a report for each district. Rather than ranking districts based on the results, the purpose of the district-level report is to identify more contextual areas of strengths and weaknesses for each district.

Results of school evaluations are analyzed by the bureaus of education in the districts as well as in the municipal office to form an overall assessment of the quality of education in the city, and to identify specific areas where performance may be weak. This information is then used to develop teacher training programs targeting the most challenging areas. The city also uses these data to identify weak or low-performing schools for additional management and financing interventions such as "entrusted management" (*weituo guanli*),[5] a policy initiative launched by the Shanghai Municipal Education Commission in 2007.

Policy Goal 3: Overseeing Service Delivery (Established)

Shanghai has established a city-level system to determine the annual school calendar along with mechanisms to monitor learning materials and physical resources at schools. Every year, the Shanghai Municipal Education Commission releases a school-year calendar that sets the beginning and end of each academic semester. For school year 2014, the fall semester started on September 1 and ended on January 31 (22 weeks). The spring semester started on February 27 and ended on June 30 (19 weeks). Municipal stipulation of instruction time facilitates coordination of textbook distribution and citywide examinations and ensures that resources are used to maximize quality learning time.

Based on the annual class instruction plan and Shanghai's school calendar, the average number of intended hours per year of total instruction time in primary schools is 765 hours. This figure is less than the Organisation for Economic Co-operation and Development (OECD) average reported in 2013 (table 4.5) but greater than in countries like Japan, Korea, and Finland. However, further investigation is warranted to better understand the qualitative differences between classroom instruction time in different countries.

Table 4.5 Average Number of Intended Instruction Hours per Year, Primary Education

Country	Average number of intended instruction hours per year
Australia	953
Canada	919
Finland	654
Japan	754
Korea, Rep.	632
Netherlands	940
OECD average	802
Shanghai[a]	**765**

Source: Organisation for Economic Co-operation and Development (OECD 2013, table D1.1).
a. Shanghai's figure is calculated on the basis of information provided by the Shanghai Municipal Education Commission in 2015.

To ensure timely delivery of learning materials, Shanghai designates a number of bookstores in the city for textbook distribution. Before the start of the school year, the Shanghai Municipal Education Commission coordinates with these bookstores on textbook selection and delivery. The bookstores then partner with schools before and during the beginning of the school year to deliver textbooks. This system allows bookstores to have quick and accurate information about demand for textbooks and respond accordingly, thus preventing delays in textbook distribution.

Several policies are in place in Shanghai to regulate the construction of safe and proper school facilities. The city has established steering committees on school construction safety at both the city and the district levels, with members from various relevant departments, specifically charged with monitoring construction progress and related expenditure. To facilitate high-quality construction of school facilities, schools in Shanghai are exempt from paying certain types of construction-related expenses, such as sewage fees and land registration fees.

Shanghai has a mechanism in place to verify teacher attendance, and substitute teachers are provided if there are absences. In Shanghai, teacher absence is not a common issue; the principal of each school closely monitors teacher attendance. In addition, the district conducts unannounced supervisory visits to schools and inspects teacher attendance. Teachers who are absent without approval are subject to possible dismissal. If a teacher is absent for a short period, other teachers of the same subject will substitute. If a teacher goes on longer-term maternity or sick leave, the school will hire substitute teachers.

According to the results of the principals' survey, the most common practice when facing a teacher shortage is to hire retired teachers as substitute teachers (61 percent of those surveyed). Sometimes, schools also borrow teachers from peer schools for a short period (17 percent). In addition, each district maintains a pool of substitute teachers who are seniors in tertiary teacher preparation programs or new graduates, who can substitute for teachers on leave with short notice. Therefore, students are guaranteed to have a teacher present in the classroom.

Policy Goal 4: Budgeting with Adequate and Transparent Information (Established)

Shanghai creates its education budget based on clear guidelines. The "Provision on Budget Management for Institutions" produced by the Shanghai Municipal Education Commission specifies the criteria for education funding. Budget allocation for each school in Shanghai follows a four-step process:

1. Each school prepares a budget including explanatory information to the district for evaluation. Every school in Shanghai prepares a three-year plan to set development goals. The development plan serves as an important basis for each school's budget proposal. Schools also take into consideration staff, enrollment, and special programs when preparing their budgets. The staff association at each school, made up of approximately 30 percent of teachers and staff, is also involved in providing suggestions and feedback in the budget preparation process. The district compiles the budgets into a master version to submit to the district's Department of Finance.
2. The Department of Finance evaluates the proposal and provides an approved estimated budget to schools with feedback.
3. Schools adjust their proposed budgets based on feedback from the Department of Finance and submit the revised versions to the district. The district again compiles the budgets to submit to the district's Department of Finance for a second round of evaluation.
4. After the district-level Departments of Finance approve the budgets of the schools within their districts, the master budget is delivered to the municipal government for approval. The approved budget is then allocated to districts, which in turn distribute the budget to district schools.

By implementing this rules-based process, not only do schools have the autonomy to reflect their needs in their proposed budgets, but the city is able to quickly respond to education expenditure needs and stay apprised of resources allocated to each school for accountability. Districts play a key role in basic education financing.

At the end of the fiscal year, the city collects data on actual education expenditure to provide information for future budget planning. In addition to the annual budget process, Shanghai also plans for education expenditures on a multiyear basis. The city engages in both three-year and five-year budget planning for education funding.

Education budgeting is based on adequate and transparent information and made available to the public. In addition to the four-step budgeting process, to ensure adequate funding for education Shanghai adheres to the national "three increases" guideline specified in the 2006 amendment to the 1986 Compulsory Education Law of the People's Republic of China: (1) the increase in education funding should be higher than the increase in the city's regular revenue; (2) per capita student funding should increase every year; and (3) teacher salaries and student per capita operational funding should increase every year.[6]

Shanghai has consistently emphasized the importance of education in its human development agenda. The municipal government's expenditure on education topped 3.5 percent of GDP in 2013. It is important to note that the relatively low rate of public expenditure on education as a share of GDP, compared with other high-performing systems (see table 4.6), can be attributed to the city's continuous economic growth along with a small school-age population, rather than an overall low level of investment. In fact, the city requires that all districts devote no less than 16 percent of their public expenditures to education. If districts have difficulty financing their budget allocations, the city will transfer funds from well-resourced districts to subsidize public education. In reality, 43 percent of the schools surveyed indicated that lack of funds has never been a reason for terminating any education initiative; 47 percent indicated that they have rarely encountered the problem; and only 9 percent have faced the problem multiple times.

Even though Shanghai devotes a smaller proportion of its GDP to education, because of its large revenue base, its total public education expenditure per student far exceeds the average for China nationwide at every level of education (table 4.7).

Public schools receive allocations for personnel and operational expenditures. Personnel expenditures cover salaries and benefits and are based on the number

Table 4.6 Public Expenditure on Education as a Share of GDP

Country or economy	Public expenditure on education as share of GDP (%)
China (2013)	4.2
Finland (2011)	6.8
Hong Kong SAR, China (2013)	3.8
Japan (2012)	3.9
Korea, Rep. (2011)	4.9
Singapore (2013)	2.9
Shanghai (2013)	3.5
United States (2011)	5.2

Sources: UNESCO Institute for Statistics 2015 (http://data.uis.unesco.org/Index.aspx?queryid=181); *China Statistical Yearbook 2014,* "2013 Public Expenditure on Education" (http://www.stats.gov.cn/tjsj/ndsj/2015/indexch.htm); Shanghai Municipal Education Commission 2015, "2013 Shanghai GDP" (http://www.stats-sh.gov.cn/sjfb/201401/266386.html).

Table 4.7 Total per Student Public Expenditure by Level of Education, 2013
U.S. Dollars

	Shanghai	China
Preprimary	3,504	1,066
Primary	3,810	1,377
Junior secondary	5,193	1,878
Senior secondary	7,861	2,109
Secondary vocational	7,300	2,281
Higher education (bachelor's degree)	8,783	4,841
Higher education (vocational)	6,094	2,759

Sources: National Bureau of Statistics of China 2013 (http://data.stats.gov.cn/easyquery.htm?cn=C01&zb=A0306&sj=2010) and *China Statistical Yearbook: Education 2013* (http://www.stats.gov.cn/tjsj/ndsj/2013/indexeh.htm).

of teachers and staff at the school. Nonsalary operational expenditures are mainly distributed in the form of a per student allocation. The Shanghai Municipal Education Commission sets annual standards for the minimum per student allocation. For example, the 2014 guidelines require the per student allocation to be no lower than RMB 1,600 for primary schools, and no lower than RMB 1,800 for secondary schools. Each district can choose to increase the amount based on its own revenue. Operational expenditures also include training fees for teachers (based on the number of teachers) and administrative expenses (such as work-related transportation, meals, and meetings). The district is responsible for making allocations for school renovation and construction. According to the survey conducted with 153 school principals, the operational budget is commonly used to cover the following items: utilities (99 percent of schools use the operational budget for this item), purchases of learning materials (90 percent), office supplies (98 percent), training (91 percent), equipment purchases (95 percent), and building and facility maintenance (94 percent).

In the funding allocation scheme, student performance is deliberately excluded from the criteria so that schools enrolling students with academic challenges are not disadvantaged. However, schools in high-revenue districts (usually in the central area of Shanghai) tend to have better education resources because these affluent districts not only have a higher absolute level of revenue but also can afford to invest more than the 16 percent threshold (established by the Shanghai municipal office).

The planned and executed municipal education budget is comprehensive and publicly available. Every year, the Shanghai municipal government releases a report to the public on the previous year's execution of the city-level budget and budget planning for the coming year, which includes a section on education. The education section covers (1) the current year's budget; (2) a summary of budget data for both revenue and expenditure; (3) the previous year's budget outturn; and (4) an explanation of the budget implications of new policy initiatives. All education expenditure information is collected, consolidated, and made available within 10 months of the end of the fiscal year. In addition, district-level budget data are available online. A number of schools also publish their planned and executed education budgets on the school website for public viewing. This prompt and comprehensive documentation presents policy makers with information on the efficiency of budget execution and allows for public monitoring. At the school level, 80 percent of schools surveyed present the school's executed budget to the staff association once or twice a year as a finance monitoring measure.

Policy Goal 5: Providing More Resources to Students Who Need Them (Established)

Shanghai has specific policies at the district and household levels to assist students from disadvantaged backgrounds with education expenses. Tuition is free for basic education (first through ninth grades) in Shanghai, and the city abolished the textbook and miscellaneous fees in 2007. All other fees for basic education, such as extracurricular activities, uniforms, and meals are determined at schools' discretion. Furthermore, to reduce the prevalence of tutoring, in 2013 the city released guidelines stipulating that schools are not allowed to offer compensated tutoring or after-school classes. Nor can public schoolteachers offer paid tutoring sessions outside the school.

Shanghai released "Advice on Program to Improve Student Nutrition at Compulsory Education Level," which allocates funding to schools to provide free lunches to students whose family incomes are below the poverty line, or whose parent(s) has a rural residence. For senior secondary (grade 10–12) expenses, poor families can apply every year for an education subsidy of between RMB 1,000 and RMB 3,000. In addition, eligible families with special economic hardships or with children with disabilities can apply for an exemption from tuition every year and receive RMB 2,000 as an annual education subsidy. These targeted assistance programs in Shanghai's education finance system provide more resources to poor families, contributing to more equal educational opportunities.

In addition to municipal policy regulations, 70 percent of the schools surveyed address educational access for children of migrant families (see box 4.1), disabled

---

Box 4.1 Education of Migrant Children in Shanghai

Because of rapidly increasing rates of urbanization and migration in China, it has been difficult for urban authorities to accommodate the basic development needs of the swelling populations of the country's big cities. For example, in Shanghai, the number of nonlocals increased from 1.7 million in 1986 to 9.6 million in 2012, swelling to almost 40 percent of the city's population (Ming 2014). In 1996, the Ministry of Education drafted the "Provisional Act Regarding the Education of School-Age Children of the Floating Population," stating that public schools had an obligation to enroll children with local residence permits. However, this requirement presented several challenges. In 2006, the revised Compulsory Education Law again emphasized the host government's responsibility for migrant children. But it also mentioned the principle of "enrollment in nearby schools." Before 2008, migrant students in Beijing and Shanghai were only entitled to public schooling if their parents could produce the "Five Licenses": temporary residence permit, proof of employment, proof of residence, certificate from the place of origin showing that the family could not provide caregiving support to its children there, and the *hukou* booklet (Ming 2014). In 2006, Human Rights Watch estimated that as many as 90 percent of migrant workers did not have all five licenses and hence had difficulty seeking public education services. The National Population and Family Planning Commission estimated in 2012 that 3.5 percent of migrant children in Beijing were not attending school; 5.1 percent of migrant children in Shanghai, and 5.3 percent of those in Guangzhou were not in school, while the national average was 2 percent.[a] Although the government of Shanghai reduced these license requirements from five to two, in Beijing, the five license requirement is still in effect and posing obstacles for public school enrollment of migrant children (Ming 2014).

box continues next page

How Shanghai Does It • http://dx.doi.org/10.1596/978-1-4648-0790-9

Box 4.1 Education of Migrant Children in Shanghai *(continued)*

The Shanghai Municipal Education Commission recognizes the importance of making sure that migrant students obtain a quality education and has therefore adopted a policy of integration. According to OECD (2010, 96), Shanghai is among the cities that have dealt with migrant children with "reason and sympathy." The municipal government is committed to providing the nine-year basic education to all Shanghai residents including eligible migrant children. As of 2015, Shanghai defines eligibility criteria as (1) one of the parents having held the Shanghai Temporary Resident Card for more than three years, and (2) one of the parents having had an employment certificate in Shanghai for two years. In addition to neighborhood public schools, Shanghai also has a program of purchasing enrollment spaces from private schools to admit eligible migrant children for free.

a. China Labour Bulletin 2013 (online). "Migrant workers and their children." http://www.clb.org.hk/en/content/migrant -workers-and-their-children.

children, and children from disadvantaged families in their school development plans. The ratio is much higher for public schools (75 percent) than for private schools (55 percent) and for rural schools (74 percent) than for urban schools (67 percent). Overall, another 27 percent address the issue in their daily work, but not in the school plans, suggesting that in practice the educational access of the disadvantaged student population is of substantial concern to schools.

Policies to address equity in basic education tend to concentrate more at the school and district levels rather than being aimed at individual students. At the district level, Shanghai implements an "education levy" to transfer resources more equitably. Under the policy, all districts collect an education tax, part of which is transferred to the municipal level. The municipal government then redistributes the proceeds of the tax to districts with poorer schools as additional education funding. Districts in the rural area of Shanghai are major beneficiaries of this policy given that they often host more socioeconomically disadvantaged students and generate lower district income revenue.

At the school level, Shanghai uses a number of financing, management, and twinning strategies aimed at improving the performance of poorly perform-ing schools. The most prominent model is the "entrusted school" management system, which involves additional financing, management, and professional sup-port from high-performing schools to low-performing schools. Unlike the charter school movement in the United States, for example, the entrusted school man-agement model often entrusts management to another high-performing school rather than to a private entity.

Financing and Management of "Entrusted Schools"
The Shanghai Municipal Education Commission has been far ahead of its coun-terparts in other provinces in ensuring equality of access to quality schools. In 1994, almost five years before the rest of the country, Shanghai eliminated the

"key school" system. The Chinese system of education had a long tradition of key schools, or public schools that received greater resources than other schools and were more selective. Shanghai requires its students to attend their local neighborhood school at the primary and lower secondary levels rather than compete for limited spots at key schools. The positive impacts of this reform included (1) no more high-stakes exams for students' entry into key schools, (2) a more inclusive and heterogeneous distribution of the student population by class and ability, and (3) alleviation of parents' stress for school choice at the primary and lower secondary levels. To further improve all children's chances to attain a high-quality education, the Shanghai Municipal Education Commission in 2007 launched a noteworthy initiative called entrusted management to provide financial and technical assistance to low-performing schools in Shanghai. This initiative was based on the findings of a school development experience in Pudong District (see box 4.2).

Entrusted schools (*weituo guanli*), a prominent approach to education financing in Shanghai, was a model specially developed to improve the quality of education in low-performing schools, particularly in rural areas.

Box 4.2 The Origin of Entrusted Management Model of Shanghai: The Pudong Experience

History: "Entrusted management" originated from the development experience of Pudong District in Shanghai. Since 2005, the government in Pudong has carried out entrusted management on a trial basis. A low-performing public school, Donggou Senior Secondary School, was entrusted to the Shanghai Education Management Consulting Center, with financial support from the government. Within four years, Donggou Senior Secondary School was transformed from a "low-tier school" to a well-recognized top-level school among the public schools. This success attracted a great deal of public attention, especially in view of the rural-urban disparity in school quality and culture in Shanghai.

Policy initiative: In 2007, the Shanghai Municipal Education Commission began to roll out this entrusted management model to more schools in the city. The newly developed model has kept the essence of the Pudong experiment. High-performing public schools or well-regarded specialized education organizations located in the center of Shanghai City may take over the management of low-performing schools, backed with financial support and monitoring from the government. In this model, while the original ownership of the entrusted low-level schools remains unchanged, the top-level schools entrusted with the low-level schools have the right to make decisions in school management and core teaching-learning practices. The focus rests on the holistic development of the school culture and improvement of the quality of education. In practice, high-level schools or specialized education organizations work together with entrusted low-level schools to develop a three-year or five-year school development plan that lays the groundwork for the long-term development of entrusted schools and helps prevent the entrusted schools from reverting to their original status.

Under this system, the municipal government devotes a special budget to provide incentives to strong schools or specialized education organizations to support weak schools through a memorandum of understanding or a contract. School leaders (usually principals) from strong schools are deployed to participate in the management of weak schools. The memorandum of understanding specifies the details of the technical assistance to be provided by the new management team. Through this pairing of school leaders, weak schools learn strategies for achieving high performance and gain capacity in school management and instructional practices. Funds are only released upon satisfactory achievement of performance indicators specified in the contract.

The pairing has been found to contribute to capacity building in weak schools. Reportedly, in 2007 the number of senior-grade teachers increased by more than 5 percent in 51 percent of the weak junior secondary schools that were involved in the entrusted management program, and increased by more than 10 percent in 29 percent of such schools (Shen 2007).

According to Tan (2013), in her detailed analysis of Shanghai's education model, the entrusted management program can take either of two formats: (1) to strengthen school leadership by replacing the school principal in a weak school, or (2) to support the existing leadership by sending good teachers. Quality is assured by periodic monitoring and evaluation by the Shanghai Education Evaluation Institute (regarded as a third-party evaluator) at the initial, middle, and final stages. The evaluation combines self-evaluation from entrusted and entrusting entities themselves along with evaluation from experts. In the self-evaluation process, the entrusting schools or organizations design the self-evaluation instrument based upon their development plan, and then evaluate themselves according to this instrument, specifying the objectives, actions, empirical evidence for these actions, outcomes, and effectiveness that correspond to each indicator. In the evaluation conducted by experts, the experts critically examine the changes over time, distill lessons learned, and point out problems to be resolved in the future.

To further increase students' chances of entering high-performing senior secondary schools, the Shanghai authorities in 2007 introduced a "quota allocation policy" (*minge fenpei fa*). Under this policy high-performing experimental schools will have to set aside a quota of 18 percent[7] of senior secondary school vacancies to all students graduating from junior secondary schools in each district. Chances of entering high-performing senior secondary schools, within the specified quota, will be based on merit and available to all students (Tan 2013).

Special Education

The World Health Organization recommends that countries provide mainstream programs and services that "address the barriers that exclude persons with disabilities from participating equally with others in any activity and service intended for the general public, such as education" (WHO and World Bank 2011, 264). Most OECD countries generally provide mainstream education services for students with special needs (box 4.3). Shanghai has special schools

Box 4.3 Special Education Provision in Other Countries

Japan

Based on specific disabilities, special education is provided in three ways: in special schools, in special classes and resource rooms within normal schools, or within the normal classroom. Whenever possible, Japanese educators try to keep students with mild to moderate learning disabilities in class and on track with their peers. Separate schools are reserved for students who cannot learn the same way as children in normal schools, including students who are blind, deaf, or otherwise handicapped. In 2003, 1.6 percent of Japanese students in primary and lower secondary school received special education. For students with minor learning difficulties, classmates are expected to help one another. This process is mutually beneficial because tutoring another student reinforces the concepts for the stronger student. Overall, the entire process reinforces the sense of community within the classroom.

Singapore

The Ministry of Education and the National Council of Social Services fund special education schools that are typically structured around the type of disability. However, there are long waiting lists for admission. Special needs education is available through the postsecondary level, where students with intellectual disabilities are prepared for the workforce through special training programs. Whenever possible, the government encourages students to join the mainstream educational system, either initially or after having met certain benchmarks in special education. To help facilitate this mainstreaming, Special Needs Officers are placed in mainstream schools to help students with conditions such as dyslexia or high-functioning autism. The ministry also announced that in the coming years, they hope to have 10 percent of all primary and secondary school teachers trained in special education. Singapore does not require students with special needs who are unable to attend a mainstream school to complete compulsory education. The Singapore government estimates that those who cannot or do not attend school comprise 0.01 percent of the population.

Korea

The Ministry of Education requires that there be at least one special school in each province to serve the estimated 2.4 percent of Korean students who need special education. The majority of special schools are comprehensive, serving students of all ages with severe handicaps. Students with mild to moderate special needs are encouraged to remain in the mainstream schools, either enrolled in special classes within the school, or in a combination of special and mainstream classes according to ability. In 2007, the Ministry of Education instituted a program intended to integrate special needs education into mainstream education as much as possible. Central components of this program were the creation of more jobs for special needs teachers in mainstream schools and professional development for mainstream teachers to prepare them to work with students with special needs. Currently, the ministry is in the process of expanding compulsory special needs education to children as young as age four, upgrading vocational opportunities for teenage special needs students, and establishing special needs support groups in colleges.

box continues next page

How Shanghai Does It • http://dx.doi.org/10.1596/978-1-4648-0790-9

Box 4.3 **Special Education Provision in Other Countries** *(continued)*

Finland

In 2010, 23.3 percent of comprehensive school students in Finland received extra instruction from a school-based Special Needs Education Teacher in the subjects in which the student needed help. Of this group, 12 percent received aid for a speech disorder, 40.5 percent received help in reading or writing, 23.7 percent for learning difficulties in mathematics, 9 percent for learning difficulties in foreign languages, 5.5 percent for adjustment difficulties or emotional disorders, and 8.9 percent for other learning difficulties. Students classified as having more intensive learning difficulties, including severely delayed development, severe handicaps, autism, dysphasia, and visual or hearing impairment (1.2 percent of the school population in 2010) were educated in a special education school. Special education teachers are important in the process of diagnosis and intervention, but it is not up to them alone to identify students. Each school has a group of staff that meets twice a month to assess the success of individual classrooms and potential concerns within classrooms. This group, comprising the principal, the school nurse, the special education teacher, the school psychologist, a social worker, and the classroom teachers, determines whether problems exist, as well as how to rectify them. If students are considered to need help beyond what the school can provide, the school helps the family find professional intervention.

Source: NCEE 2015.

for students with hearing, visual, and speech disabilities, as well as schools for mentally challenged children and those with autism. Students with disabilities or special needs do not yet commonly join mainstream education; however, the Shanghai Municipal Education Commission is working to develop formal special education pathways in mainstream and special schools, including the development of separate curricula and teaching materials (NCEE 2014). Additionally, they have established formal certificates for special education teacher training and have been working toward setting standards for preservice teacher training in special education.

In 2014, the commission announced plans to offer individualized education to children with disabilities who receive medical care. This plan comprised a comprehensive approach integrating expertise from teachers and doctors to design a unique curriculum for each child based on his or her needs. It involves assignment of community doctors to local schools to provide regular support to teachers and parents of children with special needs. As of 2014, Shanghai was reported to have more than 9,000 registered disabled students with conditions including blindness, deafness, autism, learning difficulties, and Down's syndrome (NCEE 2014). Shanghai could consider establishing and strengthening a comprehensive education system that allows students with special needs to be systematically integrated into the same classrooms as nondisabled children, to the extent appropriate, so that all children, as they become adults, are fully engaged with society and, later, the labor market.

Policy Goal 6: Managing Resources Efficiently (Advanced)

Systems are in place to verify the use of educational resources. It is important to review education expenditures against the planned education budget, to hold actors in the school finance system accountable for their use of resources. Under the "Regulations on Primary and Secondary School Finance," schools in Shanghai must use allocated funding within defined categories. All purchases made by the school need to be supported by documentation and receipts. Because teacher salaries are a major education expenditure, a personnel database can help track related expenses. Shanghai has a personnel database that is updated comprehensively at least once every year. The database is also updated whenever a teacher is hired or dismissed at the school level because the school needs to report the procedure to the district immediately for approval. Although this procedure allows personnel changes to be accounted for promptly, more regular updates of the personnel database might be helpful along with checks against the payroll database to make adjustments in salary distributions.

In addition to teacher salaries, capital cost for construction of school facilities is a major educational expenditure. The legal and regulatory framework for school construction requires Shanghai to use an open competition method for procurement. School construction contracts are all based on open bidding. Each district in Shanghai has a specific office that helps schools with the public bidding process and receives complaints. This transparent process ensures the efficient use of funding for school construction and is less conducive to corruption.

Education expenditures are audited regularly in Shanghai. Under the "Regulations on Primary and Secondary School Finance," schools are required to submit reports on education expenditure and revenue to district and municipal Departments of Finance every year. According to the survey results, 98 percent and 96 percent of the schools have specific policies on finance management and capital management, respectively, to ensure strict financial compliance. In addition to financial reporting, schools are required to have internal financial supervision of the budget, revenue, expenditures, monetary transfers, and the validity of data on enrollment and teachers. Those internal audits can provide education authorities with timely information on each school's management and allocation of funds. The municipal and district Audit Offices also carry out external audits of school expenditure and revenues to verify the use of resources throughout the year. Schools that fail internal or external audits receive legal sanctions.

Summary

The application of SABER–Finance paints a positive picture of public education financing in Shanghai, with ratings at "established" or "advanced" for the six policy goals of (1) ensuring basic conditions for learning, (2) monitoring learning conditions and outcomes, (3) overseeing service delivery, (4) budgeting with adequate and transparent information, (5) providing more resources to students who need them, and (6) managing resources efficiently.

Shanghai's public investment in education, about 3.5 percent of GDP, is slightly lower than the 4.2 percent average nationwide. However, the key objectives of public finance for education in Shanghai clearly focus on ensuring a minimum level of learning conditions and standards from basic infrastructure to teachers and other inputs. Learning outcomes are monitored, but Shanghai deliberately no longer uses student learning outcomes as an explicit financing measure. If there is any link between school evaluation and financing of schools, Shanghai strives to undertake school evaluation in a comprehensive fashion through the "Green Indicators of Academic Quality of Primary and Secondary School Students." Poorly performing schools and districts are provided with additional fiscal transfers as well as specific support arrangements, such as the entrusted school model, which provides management, pedagogical, and financial assistance.

Shanghai could potentially improve the provision of information and communications technology (ICT) in schools and reduce class size further. ICT includes the provision of basic information technology infrastructure for teaching and EMIS activities. Although 95 percent of schools indicate that their student registration profiles (basic student background information) are completely or mostly in an electronic format, only 72 percent report that their student growth profiles (which include more detailed information on student achievement over the years) and 67 percent report that their teacher professional development profiles are completely or mostly in an electronic format. Additional investment in upgrading ICT and reducing class size will inevitably have implications for the education budget.

Another key feature of Shanghai's public financing for education is a focus on improving poorly performing schools. In fact, unlike many school systems in which top schools are rewarded, Shanghai does not offer financing incentives for well-performing schools; instead, multiple financing and management approaches target low-performing schools. These mechanisms include additional fiscal transfers to low-performing districts, the entrusted school management system, and the practice of reserving a certain proportion of seats in the highly sought-after model senior secondary schools especially for graduates of low-performing schools.

Because of the boom in the population of migrant children during the past decade, policy awareness of the requirement to meet the needs of "disadvantaged" students and pockets of the population has been heightened. Shanghai has been proactive in enacting new policies and approaches to expanding education services to migrant and other disadvantaged children. However, further efforts can be made—the current eligibility criteria of three years of residency and employment may be too stringent and need to be relaxed to allow more migrant children to enroll in local public or government-sponsored private schools and receive free compulsory education. The practice of requiring poor children to update their poverty status every year may also carry too much stigma for the children and their families.

Special education is another area with room for improvement. Shanghai has special schools for students with hearing, visual, and speech disabilities, as well as schools for mentally challenged and autistic children. However, because the city has not yet developed an integrated education environment, students with disabilities or special needs do not commonly join mainstream education classrooms.

Shanghai would benefit from a comprehensive household survey to acquire a full picture of migrant and special education children's educational needs and constraints. For example, it would be important to understand the burden on migrant and other disadvantaged populations caused by private education expenditures, and the disparities in total education expenditures between residents and nonresidents, and between poor and more well-to-do populations.

Finally, Shanghai could further improve the performance-based incentive system for teachers and for low-performing schools.

Notes

1. Japan Ministry of Internal Affairs and Communications (2007). Structure of the "u-Japan Policy Package." http://www.soumu.go.jp/menu_seisaku/ict/u-japan_en /new_plcy_pckg.html.

2. Singapore Government (2015). E-Gov. http://www.egov.gov.sg/about-egov-introduct ion;jsessionid=7559CB3C3647CA0C9CD859B01C519124.

3. Korea Agency for Digital Opportunity and Promotion (2007). "Korea's Informatization Policy to Deliver ICT Use in Everyday Life." http://unpan1.un.org/intradoc/groups /public/documents/unpan/unpan036280.pdf.

4. For a long time, most Chinese provinces required separate tests for graduation and for selection into higher levels of education. Many provinces have recently decided to merge the two tests into one, as Shanghai has done.

5. This model requires urban districts in Shanghai, which tend to have developed better-performing schools and richer educational resources, to assist relatively weaker or underperforming schools in the outskirts or rural districts. High-performing schools may even be paired with relatively low performing schools in the same district.

6. The Central People's Government of the People's Republic of China (2006), "People's Republic of China Compulsory Education Law" (http://www.gov.cn/flfg/2006 -06/30/content_323302.htm); and Shanghai Education Commission (2006), "Notice of Strengthening Reform of Guarantee Mechanism of Rural Compulsory Education Fund" (http://www.shmec.gov.cn/attach/xxgk/2495.htm).

7. An alternate figure of 30 percent was provided by Shanghai's education officials.

References

Ming, H. 2014. "Migrant Workers' Children and China's Future: The Educational Divide." *Asia-Pacific Journal* 12 (9): 4. http://japanfocus.org/-Holly_H_-Ming/4084/article .html.

Ministry of Education of China. 2014. "Feedbacks of National Education Supervision Group on Compulsory Education Balanced Development of 17 Counties of

Shanghai." *Beijing*. http://www.moe.edu.cn/publicfiles/business/htmlfiles/moe
/s5987/201403/166009.html.

NCEE (Center on International Education Benchmarking). 2014. "Shanghai-China:
Education for All—Student Support Systems." Center on International Education
Benchmarking, Washington, DC. http://www.ncee.org/programs-affiliates/center-on
-international-education-benchmarking/top-performing-countries/shanghai-china
/shanghai-china-education-for-all/.

———. 2015. "Top Performing Countries." Center on International Education
Benchmarking, Washington, DC. http://www.ncee.org/programs-affiliates/center-on
-international-education-benchmarking/top-performing-countries/.

OECD (Organisation for Economic Co-operation and Development). 2010. "Shanghai
and Hong Kong: Two Distinct Examples of Education Reform in China." In *Strong
Performers and Successful Reformers in Education: Lessons from PISA for the United
States*. Paris: OECD Publishing. http://www.oecd.org/countries/hongkongchina
/46581016.pdf.

———. 2012. Database PISA-2012. OECD, Paris. https://pisa2012.acer.edu.au
/downloads.php.

———. 2013. *Education at a Glance 2013: OECD Indicators*. Paris: OECD Publishing.

Shanghai Municipal Education Commission. 2011. "Opinions on Quality Indicators of
Primary and Secondary Education of Shanghai." http://www.shmec.gov.cn/attach
/xxgk/5108.doc.

Shen, X. 2007. *Shanghai Education*. Singapore: Cengage Learning Asia. http://www
.worldscientific.com/worldscibooks/10.1142/t011.

Tan, C. 2013. *Learning from Shanghai: Lessons on Achieving Educational Success*. Springer
Verlag, Singapur. http://www.springer.com/us/book/9789814021869.

Vegas, E., and C. Coffin. 2013. "What Matters Most for School Finance: A Framework
Paper." SABER Working Paper, World Bank, Washington, DC. http://wbgfiles
.worldbank.org/documents/hdn/ed/saber/supporting_doc/Background/FIN
/Framework_School_Finance.pdf.

WHO and World Bank (World Health Organization and World Bank). 2011. *World Report
on Disability*. Geneva: WHO.

CHAPTER 5

Balancing Autonomy and Accountability

Introduction

The Autonomy and Accountability module of the World Bank's Systems Approach for Better Education Results (SABER–School Autonomy and Accountability) documents and analyzes school-based management policies aimed at increasing autonomy and accountability at the school level and within the education system in Shanghai. It measures the extent to which education policies enable school autonomy and accountability. It uses five indicators to assess the degree of autonomy and accountability: (1) school autonomy in budget planning and approval, (2) school autonomy in personnel management, (3) participation of the school council in school finance, (4) assessment of school and student performance, and (5) school accountability (table 5.1).

School autonomy is a form of school-based management in which schools are given decision-making authority over all or some aspects of their operations, often with the involvement and collaboration of parents and communities, including budget management; the hiring, transfer, and firing of personnel; and the assessment of teachers and pedagogical practices (Demas and Arcia 2015; Arcia et al. 2011). The degree of autonomy or specific aspects of autonomy, and the involvement of stakeholders, vary greatly from one school system to another.

School accountability is the acceptance of responsibility and being answerable for one's actions. Accountability measures can include (1) complying with the rules and regulations of school governance, (2) reporting to those with oversight authority over the school, and (3) linking rewards and sanctions to expected results (Demas and Arcia 2015; Arcia et al. 2011).

Based on the SABER rubric for School Autonomy and Accountability, Shanghai was rated "established" in all policy goals except for *role of the school council in school governance* and *school accountability*, where it was rated "emerging."

Table 5.1 SABER–School Autonomy and Accountability, Shanghai

Policy and resource framework (Goals and indicators)	SABER score
Level of autonomy in planning and management of the school budget	●●●○
1. Legal authority over management of the operational budget	●●●○
2. Legal authority over management of nonteaching staff salaries	●●●○
3. Legal authority over management of teacher salaries	●●●○
4. Legal authority to raise additional funds for the school	●●○○
5. Collaborative budget planning	●●●○
Level of autonomy in personnel management	●●●○
1. Autonomy in teacher appointment and deployment decision	●●●○
2. Autonomy in nonteaching staff appointment and deployment decision	●●●○
3. Autonomy in school principal appointment and deployment decision	●●●○
Role of the school council in school governance	●●○○
1. Participation of the school council in budget preparation	●●●○
2. Participation of the school council in financial oversight	●●●●
3. Participation of the school council in personnel management	●○○○
4. Participation of the school council in school activities	●○○○
5. Participation of the school council in learning inputs	●○○○
6. Transparency in community participation	●○○○
School and student assessment	●●●○
1. Existence and frequency of school assessments	●●●○
2. Use of school assessments for making school adjustments	●●●●
3. Existence and frequency of standardized student assessments	●●●●
4. Use of standardized student assessments for making school adjustments	●●●○
5. Publication of student assessments	●●●○
School accountability	●●○○
1. Guidelines for the use of results of student assessments	●●●○
2. Analysis of school and student performance	●●○○
3. Degree of financial accountability at the central, regional, municipal, local, and school levels	●●●○
4. Degree of accountability in school operations	●●●○
5. Degree of learning accountability	●○○○

Note: Scoring rubric: Latent (●○○○), Emerging (●●○○), Established (●●●○), Advanced (●●●●).
SABER = Systems Approach for Better Education Results.

Policy Goal 1: Level of Autonomy in Planning and Management of the School Budget (Established)

School budgets are prepared and proposed by schools, reviewed by the districts, and finally approved by the municipal government. The "Provision on Budget Management for Institutions" produced by the Shanghai Municipal Education Commission stipulates a four-step process for budget preparation and allocation (see SABER–Finance in chapter 4 for the detailed process).

In this collaborative process, schools take the initiative to prepare their operational budgets, taking into consideration the number of students and staff and the school's program offerings. This process allows schools to make budget requests that are tailored to their needs and potentially increases the efficiency of financial resource allocations. The district Department of Finance makes recommendations on revising individual school's budgets, and the municipal government grants final approval of the budget. Therefore, two layers of monitoring ensure that school budgets are appropriately designed. After receiving the approved budget, schools have the autonomy to execute the budget within the defined categories (see SABER–Finance for detailed categories). For example, the personnel-related budget is based on the number of teachers and staff and is distributed to pay employees' salaries; training fees are used exclusively for teacher professional development.

Public schools in Shanghai are not allowed to fund-raise, but they have the right to request changes in their operational budgets under a number of circumstances, such as unexpected accidents or changes and changes in school finance policies.

Schools in Shanghai have some, but limited, influence on teacher pay. The central government of China, the city, and the school all participate in regulating the salaries of public school teachers hired in the *bian zhi* system (box 5.1). The salary for teaching staff consists of base salary and performance-based salary (70 percent of the wage bill is for base salaries and an additional 30 percent is to be distributed for merit-based incentives). The central government released guidelines for setting both components. Overall, the Teachers Law (1993) stipulates that teachers' average salary should be equal to or higher than the average salary of civil servants in China. The base salary standards follow the national

---

Box 5.1 The *Bian Zhi* System of China

Being a teacher has long been considered the equivalent of having an "iron rice bowl" in China—an occupation with job security and a stable salary and benefits. Although teachers in public schools are not officially considered civil servants in China, they are contracted by the government under the *bian zhi* system (some private schools also contract teachers under this system). *Bian zhi* is similar to the concept of lifelong tenure. A teacher has to pass a specific exam and obtain approval from the district Department of Education to be granted a *bian zhi*. Teachers with a *bian zhi* are entitled to medical benefits, a housing stipend, and pensions, while temporary or substitute teachers do not have such privileges. According to "Advice on Creating Standards for Primary and Secondary Teachers and Bian Zhi Establishment," the ratio of teachers and staff who have *bian zhi* to students should be 1:19 at the primary level and 1:13.5 at the lower secondary level in urban areas.

Major cities such as Shanghai and Beijing recently decided to end the lifelong tenure of teachers. All basic education teachers in Shanghai now have to renew their teacher certification and be evaluated once every five years. Teachers need to have five consecutive renewals to obtain tenure. This initiative gives the government and schools more leverage in improving teacher performance by exerting pressure on teachers to be more dedicated to teaching.

"Primary and Secondary Teachers Salary Standards" (1988). Instruction for the performance-based salary component is set forth in "Guidance on the Implementation of Performance Pay at Basic Education Level." The municipal government has autonomy to decide on the specific standards for the base salary, that is 70 percent of the wage budget, in accordance with local living standards and economic development. Individual schools decide on how to distribute the remaining 30 percent of the wage budget for merit-based incentives. This three-party mechanism ensures that all teachers are guaranteed a competitive salary level, while giving schools a degree of autonomy to provide teachers with an incentive for better performance.

Globally, schools continue to have limited autonomy in determining teacher remuneration. According to a 2013 Organisation for Economic Co-operation and Development (OECD) report on governance, assessments, and account-ability, in most countries and economies, very few individual schools have sig-nificant influence over teachers' salaries. On average across OECD countries, about 70 percent or more of students are in schools whose principals reported that only national or regional education authorities (or both) have considerable responsibility for establishing teachers' starting salaries and determining teach-ers' salary increases (OECD 2013). In contrast, school principals and teachers seem to have greater responsibility for decisions related to selecting and hiring teachers, dismissing teachers, formulating the school budget, and deciding on budget allocations within the school (OECD 2013). A similar trend is observed in schools in China.

Schools in Shanghai have more say in determining the salaries of nonteaching staff. Under the overall guidelines released by the central government, "Primary and Secondary Teachers and Staff Salary System Reform Plan" (1985), the salary standards for nonteaching staff should be based on the salary standards for state administrative staff and the salary standards for teachers. Using the guidelines released by the central government as a minimum standards reference, the municipal government and schools have the discretion to create more specific standards for nonteaching staff salaries.

Comparing Private and Public Schools

In Shanghai, the school survey results provide a glimpse into principals' actual level of autonomy. Table 5.2 compares results of surveys with 153 school principals from public and private schools, demonstrating that, as in many other countries, private school principals in Shanghai generally have a higher level of autonomy than public school principals do. However, public schools in Shanghai also enjoy a fair amount of autonomy, especially in personnel management. The area with the lowest autonomy in the public schools is the ability to raise funds.

According to OECD (2013), schools within a country or an economy show varying degrees of autonomy in allocating resources. This within-country variation was found to be fairly low in Belgium, Germany, Greece, Ireland, Romania, and Turkey, where school principals reported similar levels of autonomy in allocating resources. However, in Chile; the Czech Republic;

Table 5.2 Level of Autonomy, Public and Private School Principals (N = 153)
percent

Area of autonomy	Yes		Only on paper		No	
	Public	Private	Public	Private	Public	Private
Authority to set and manage salaries of teachers and staff	26	74	35	16	39	11
Authority to set and manage benefits of teachers and staff	63	84	30	11	7	5
Authority to raise funds	11	37	8	11	81	53
Authority to create financial budget	71	79	22	11	8	11
Authority to recruit teachers	77	92	18	8	5	—
Authority to dismiss teachers	17	74	49	26	35	—

Note: — = not available.

Indonesia; Macao SAR, China; Peru; the Slovak Republic; the United Arab Emirates; and the United Kingdom, the report shows that some schools are permitted to allocate resources whereas for other schools these decisions are made by national or regional education authorities. Notably, in virtually all participating countries or economies, private schools tend to have more autonomy in allocating resources than public schools. Similarly, in most participating countries or economies upper secondary schools tend to have more autonomy in allocating resources than do lower secondary schools.

Policy Goal 2: Level of Autonomy of Personnel Management (Established)

In Shanghai, schools have different levels of autonomy for appointing and dismissing teachers. In some districts, schools can post positions and hire candidates directly; these candidates then participate in the district-level exam to apply for *bian zhi*. In some districts, candidates need to pass the district-level *bian zhi* eligibility exam before they are able to apply for school-level positions. However, a small number of districts (mostly in rural Shanghai) allow schools to recruit teachers on their own, based on candidates' background and school needs. If participating in a school-level recruitment process, all teacher candidates must be interviewed and conduct a mock teaching session organized by the school, in addition to having the necessary academic qualifications (three-year tertiary college degree for primary school teachers and four-year bachelor's degree for secondary school teachers) and a teacher certificate. Schools do not need to receive approval from the municipal level for review of teacher appointments, but they do need to coordinate closely with the district Department of Education to ensure that hired teachers can receive *bian zhi* from the district. Based on the survey results, 81 percent of principals have actual authority to hire teachers (77 percent for public schools and 92 percent for private schools); 16 percent have only notional authority; and 4 percent have no such authority. The autonomy to dismiss teachers appears to be more limited: 31 percent have actual authority (17 percent for public schools and 74 percent for private schools), 43 percent have notional authority, and 26 percent have no such authority.

Teacher transfers are not common in Shanghai. Each district has the authority to establish guidelines on transferring teachers. For example, in Qingpu District of Shanghai, schools report their teacher hiring needs to the district. The district compiles this information and publicizes it to all teachers in the district. Interested teachers are encouraged to submit applications for transfer to the original and receiving schools. After successful application to both schools, the district Department of Education grants final approval for the transfers. Usually only teachers with *bian zhi* can apply to transfer. The teacher's *bian zhi* and the affiliated benefits can be preserved with the transfer.

Although there is no specific policy with regard to nonteaching staff, such as administrative, maintenance, and security staff, the hiring and deployment process is generally more flexible. Candidates apply for open nonteaching positions announced by individual schools; schools have the autonomy to conduct interviews and make appointments.

Shanghai has no uniform municipal-level policy on the appointment and deployment of principals, but districts have the authority to establish their own processes. For example, in the district of Changning, schools recommend qualified teachers and administrators as candidates for the principal position every two years. The group of candidates recommended by the schools form a cohort of potential candidates. They receive regular training in preparation to be principals. Furthermore, Shanghai is developing a four-grade career advancement rating system for school principals. Principals will be evaluated for promotion to a higher grade based on their professional knowledge and management of schools. The promotion not only comes with a higher salary, but it also builds the principal's reputation for future advancement, thus serving as an effective principal performance incentive.

Policy Goal 3: Role of the School Council in School Governance (Emerging)

School management and the role of the school council are conceptualized and implemented differently in China and Shanghai. Public schools are legally the responsibility of principals. Public schools are not mandated to have school councils as part of the management structure. The system of principal responsibility is key to school management in China and has several components: (1) the principal, (2) the (political) party secretary and party committee, (3) a teacher and staff representative committee, and (4) parent-teacher associations.

Complementing the principal responsibility system is the parallel party management system. All public entities in China also have a party secretary; this person is an integral part of school management jointly with the school principal. The party secretary and the party committee of every public school participate in decision making concerning major school events. Together, they are responsible for moral and political education and alignment with party principles. Another key mechanism for school management is the teacher and staff representative committee, which is democratically elected and participates in a range of decision-making issues. The primary areas for decision making include formation of the school charter, development plans, annual work plans, main reforms, cultivation of school culture and spirit, personnel, teacher development plan and implementation, allocation of teacher and staff performance pay, annual budget, main construction projects, school safety regulations, admission and graduation recommendations, international exchanges, and so on.

In making major school decisions, principals propose topics and initially conceptualize strategies and plans in consultation with the party secretary, followed by extensive consultation within the school. If the principal and party secretary do not reach consensus on the main direction and approach, the discussions in the teacher and staff representative committee will be delayed. When the principal and party secretary agree, a teacher and staff management meeting will be called and chaired by the school principal to discuss the topic (Shanghai Municipal Education Commission 2011).

Since 2012 and as part of national and municipal efforts to modernize the education system, China and Shanghai have published guidelines for the establishment of parent-teacher associations (PTAs), including detailed terms of reference, eligibility criteria, composition, election process, and duration of the term. The rights and responsibilities of PTAs have largely been confined to facilitating and supporting school management, plus parent and home education of children. The terms of reference make no provision for PTAs to intervene in the teaching and learning operations of schools, although one clause does provide for PTAs to offer input to teacher evaluations.

PTA members commonly include parents and school principals; 46 percent of the schools in the survey also include teachers. According to the surveyed principals ($N = 153$), the main responsibilities of PTAs include (1) promoting communication and collaboration between schools and parents, (2) participating in and monitoring school management, and (3) supporting teaching and learning.

For private schools, the Private Education Promotion Law (2003) requires and guides the establishment and implementation of school councils in private schools. The law requires private schools to establish school councils with decision-making power (see table 5.3 for key responsibilities of school councils and principals). The council, headed by the chairman, should consist of at least five members, including the school founder, principal, teacher representatives, and staff representatives. One-third of the council members need to have at least five years of work experience in education. The survey results correspond with the policy: the school councils of the majority of the 39 private schools in the survey include the school principal (97 percent) and teacher representatives (95 percent); the school councils of 82 percent of the schools also include prominent members of the local community.

Table 5.3 Key Responsibilities—Private School Board and Principal

School board	Principal
1. Appoint and dismiss the principal	1. Implement the decisions made by the school council
2. Modify the school charter and develop school regulations	2. Implement school development plan; prepare annual work plan, school budget, and school regulations
3. Set school development plan and approve annual work plan	3. Appoint and remove school teachers and staff; implement rewards and sanctions
4. Raise operational funds; review and audit the budget and final expenditure report	4. Organize pedagogical and research activities; ensure education quality
5. Determine salary and *bian zhi* quota of teachers and staff	5. Manage daily school operations
6. Determine the division, merger, or closure of school campuses	6. Other responsibilities delegated by the school council
7. Decide other important matters	

Source: China's Private Education Promotion Law (2003).

Table 5.4 School Board Involvement in Private Schools, Data from Principal Survey (N = 153)

Question: Are your school boards generally involved in the following school affairs?	Percent of respondents answering "yes"
Appointment and dismissal of school principal	95
Budget preparation	71
Budget supervision	84
School development plan creation	79
Fund-raising	45
Teaching-related matters	21

In Shanghai, the school council is responsible for raising operational funds for the private school. The principal has final responsibility for preparing the school budget, while the school council has legal oversight authority on budget issues (table 5.4). The Private Education Promotion Law gives school councils legal recognition and the authority to audit and review the school budget.

The school council does not have the legal right to appoint, transfer, or remove teachers. However, it does have the right to determine teachers' salary levels and *bian zhi* quota. The principal has the responsibility to appoint and remove teachers and staff.

Each private school might have its own procedure given that there is no city-level policy, guideline, or manual regulating participation of the community or the school council in school activities and learning inputs. Nor does any city-level document exist on the election terms of council members. Private schools do receive guidance and support from the Office of Private Education of the Shanghai Municipal Education Commission. Table 5.4 shows the involvement of school councils in the operation of private schools as indicated by the survey.

School councils (or "boards" for Shanghai's private schools) are viewed as an important element in SABER–School Autonomy and Accountability's rubric. An advanced score on this policy goal encompasses the following aspects:

- School councils have a voice in the planning and preparation of the budget at the school level and, depending on the law, may share responsibility with the school principal.
- School councils have the legal right to oversee appointments, removals, or transfers of teachers; the legal authority to voice an opinion; and legal oversight on all learning inputs to the classroom.
- Formal instructions, manuals, and mandates are available for organizing volunteers to plan, implement, and evaluate school activities.
- There are provisions for regularly scheduled elections of school council members and defined term limits and guidelines for calling general meetings.

With such authority, school councils can serve as a bridge that connects school administrators with parents, community members, and students. Through school councils, parents and community members are able to exercise power on school management issues, focus on the improvement of learning tailored to students' needs, and hold schools accountable for their decisions. The model of local cooperation and local accountability has the potential for improving teacher performance and student learning outcomes.

In Shanghai, school-based management or autonomy in public schools is clearly more at the level of principals and party secretaries than school councils. Public schools do not have school councils but follow the principal responsibility system, whereby principals make key delegated decisions, usually in consultation with party secretaries and increasingly in consultation with teacher-staff associations. The involvement of the larger community and parents directly in the management of school affairs is still rare in Shanghai, except in private schools. PTAs are often operational now, even in public schools, since 2012 with the government's efforts to modernize the education system. However, PTAs are a relatively new phenomenon and currently play only a limited role in school management.

Policy Goal 4: School and Student Assessment (Established)

As mentioned in chapter 4 on school financing, there are currently two types of school assessments or evaluations in Shanghai: (1) the regular annual school supervisory visit, which is conducted by each district's Education Supervision Office; and (2) the sample-based "Green Indicators of Academic Quality of Primary and Secondary School Students," which also includes a module on student assessment.

Results of school evaluations are analyzed by the bureaus of education in the districts as well as in the municipal office to form an overall assessment of the quality of education in the city and in each of the districts, and also to identify specific areas where performance may be weak. This information is then used to develop specific teacher training programs targeting the most challenging curriculum areas. The city also uses this information to identify the weak or low-performing schools for additional management and financing interventions, such as "entrusted" management (see chapter 4 for an explanation of entrusted management).

City- and nationwide student achievement assessments take place annually to provide a picture of student learning outcomes. As mentioned in previous chapters, all students take the graduation examinations at the end of ninth grade (city level) to progress to the next level. This exam also serves as a selection test into high schools. At the end of twelfth grade, students take a college entrance examination (*gao kao*), which will determine whether and where a student will go to college.

The data from these assessments help policy makers track trends in student learning outcomes. Policy makers also have access to the assessment data disaggregated by district and by school, and each school has student-specific performance scores. The wide scope of information available to policy makers facilitates more effective and targeted use of resources for improvement of education quality. Unfortunately, because these tests are also placement or selection tests for the higher levels of education, they have become high-stakes tests.

Shanghai's education assessment system has made significant efforts to deemphasize assessment results. To achieve a balanced and equitable education system that is not test driven, the government has explicitly decreed under the "Regulations on Protection of Minors in Shanghai" that schools cannot organize any assessments to select students in their transition from primary to lower secondary school. Although the city sets municipal-level targets for completion and progression to promote overall achievement, schools are not evaluated based on their students' scores or rate of enrollment in high schools. Nor do schools have official access to the performance of individual students on the standardized assessments to avoid extra pressure placed on students to obtain a high score. In practice, schools adopt various measures to reduce students' academic burden. Out of the schools surveyed, 94 percent have undergone reforms to increase teaching effectiveness and reduce the amount of homework; 62 percent have issued regulations on the amount of homework teachers can assign to students and carry out regular homework inspections; and 77 percent have investigated the issue and made adjustments accordingly.

Policy Goal 5: School Accountability (Emerging)

Both national and municipal guidelines for the use of student assessments results are in place. The national "Advice on Relieving School Burden and Implementing Quality Education in Primary and Secondary Schools" emphasizes the importance of designing innovative assessments and building a comprehensive assessment system to evaluate basic education quality. At the municipal level, the

Shanghai Municipal Education Commission's "Advice on Regulating Teaching and Implementing Quality Education in Primary and Secondary Schools" strives toward a holistic assessment framework that does not heavily emphasize student assessment results. The document stipulates that no district-level exam should be carried out for students in first through third grades. For students in fourth through eighth grades, only one district-level academic assessment can be carried out every year with a random selection of no more than 30 percent of the student population.

Both guidelines are publicly available online. They call for schools to actively communicate with the parents and the community and keep them informed of matters related to school and student development through mechanisms such as phone hotlines and online communities. As revealed in the school surveys, 99 percent of schools have created a public bulletin board either at the school or online to distribute relevant information. Furthermore, to facilitate public monitoring, every district in Shanghai hosts an office that receives parents' complaints on schools. At the municipal level, parents can call a hotline number to report school complaints to the Shanghai Municipal Education Commission. Verified complaints will lead to inspection and potential sanctions to the school. The availability of those public channels allows parents and the community to exercise monitoring power and provide feedback on school performance.

Shanghai analyzes standardized student assessment results at the city level. However, the goal of the analysis is not to compare schools with each other, but rather to understand overall progress and trends of student outcomes in the city. Therefore, while some city-level educational statistics, such as the graduation rate, may be announced to the public, the results of the detailed analysis are not available to parents or to the general public. Individual students' standardized assessment results are only available to the students themselves.

Shanghai's educational system exhibits a high degree of financial accountability at multiple levels. Holding schools accountable for their own financial management ensures the efficient use of resources for quality education. Schools in Shanghai have to strictly comply with the national "Elementary and Secondary School Finance Policy," which sets out detailed rules on the management of budget, revenue, expenditures, surpluses, and capital assets. Failure to comply leads to legal sanctions. All schools need to submit thorough expenditure reports at the end of the academic year for review. Based on the national policy, schools also create their own regulations to streamline the financial management process.

For private schools specifically, Shanghai has released "Guidelines on Financial Management for Private Schools in Shanghai" and "Accounting Methods for Private Schools in Shanghai." The two documents include specific rules for financial management and transparency, reporting requirements to an oversight authority, and the consequences for failure to comply. All private schools must submit a yearly financial report within four months of the end of the year to the Department of Education for review.

How Shanghai Does It • http://dx.doi.org/10.1596/978-1-4648-0790-9

Regulations are in place for enforcing accountability in school operations. The Compulsory Education Law (1986) and "Regulation Rules for Primary School Management" lay out the rules for all aspects of school operation, including the management of enrollment, teaching practices, personnel, administration, facilities, and sanitation, and the procedure for reporting to the overseeing authority. In addition, under "Advice on Relieving School Burden and Implementing Quality Education in Primary and Secondary Schools," schools are required to publicize their annual curriculum plans on their bulletin boards and websites two weeks after the start of the academic year. This information is open to parents who may offer feedback and suggestions through PTAs, social media, or other grievance-redress platforms.

In Shanghai, schools are not allowed to publish student assessment results to the public under "Regulations on Protection of Minors in Shanghai." This policy is in place to avoid overemphasis on student scores; eliminate school rankings; and reduce exam pressure on students, teachers, and schools.

A number of policies regulate the pedagogical autonomy of schools in Shanghai. Although the central government is responsible for setting policies and guiding and monitoring matters related to textbook selection under the "Rules for Textbook Selection (Draft)," the municipal government has the authority to choose textbooks. In certain cases, schools that pilot experimental projects or have special needs can apply to choose textbooks on their own.

The "Standards for Regular Primary and Secondary School Teaching Equipment" in Shanghai specify the type and volume of teaching equipment for different subjects at the primary and secondary school levels, although schools have the autonomy to adjust the equipment list based on individual needs.

The central, municipal, and school levels are all engaged in designing the curriculum. At the central level, the Ministry of Education sets overall curriculum standards for all subjects. Shanghai has released the subject-specific "Curriculum Plan for Regular Elementary and Secondary Schools in Shanghai." Schools have the autonomy to design 30 percent of the curriculum as school-based curriculum according to each school's strengths and the area of their curricular focus. In practice, the 153 schools surveyed have developed, on average, 25 school-based courses in the past three years and offer 4 such courses every week. In addition to the school-based curriculum, schools provide students with a wide range of curriculum resources, including lectures from outside speakers (75 percent), extracurricular activities organized at the school level (98 percent) and at the district and city level (83 percent), and online coursework (25 percent).

Furthermore, teachers have a certain level of pedagogical autonomy: 42 percent of the schools surveyed allow teachers to make some pedagogical modifications after the curriculum is confirmed, and 39 percent of the schools encourage teachers to make innovative teaching efforts. Only 3 percent require teachers to strictly follow the curriculum standards with a uniform teaching process.

The school calendar is established at the city level. Every year, the Shanghai Municipal Education Commission releases a school year calendar that establishes the start and end of each semester. For example, the 2014 school year starts on September 1, and the first semester ends on January 30 (22 weeks). The second semester starts on February 27 and ends on June 30 (19 weeks).

However, there are no explicit policies and mechanisms for learning accountability toward stakeholders in the form of public forums. Communities and parents tend to trust the education professionals in the management of professional affairs and educational institutions.

Summary

The SABER–School Autonomy and Accountability rubric was used to assess the extent to which education policies enable school autonomy and accountability. Five sets of indicators assess the degree of autonomy and accountability in the following dimensions: (1) school autonomy in budget planning and approval, (2) school autonomy in personnel management, (3) participation of the school council in school finance, (4) assessment of school and student performance, and (5) school accountability.

Overall, the Shanghai system can be described as one with controlled school autonomy and a high degree of professional accountability in addition to compliance with regulations and rules. Contrary to most beliefs that the Chinese system is highly centralized, a fair amount of autonomy is embedded within the education system. The fiscal decentralization policy that began in the 1980s allowed Shanghai to be responsible for the provision of compulsory education as well as the tertiary education institutions affiliated with the city. Furthermore, Shanghai was granted curriculum autonomy for basic education. Therefore, Shanghai has full autonomy to finance and manage education affairs within the city, under the overall direction of the central government. Given that most of the education policies promulgated by the central government are broadly framed, Shanghai can exercise a high degree of autonomy within those policies. And because most of the key education targets and standards are set as minimum thresholds that can be exceeded, to date Shanghai has always surpassed them.

Within Shanghai, schools also operate with a high level of autonomy in consultation with districts and the municipality. In principle, schools determine their budgets within the parameters set by the municipality. Schools also can customize 30 percent of their curricula. Principals further possess teacher hiring and firing authority although they rarely exercise this authority, and if they do, they do so in consultation with district offices. Schools can manage their own operating budgets, including the hiring and firing of nonteaching staff. About 30 percent of total teacher salaries is also managed at the school level to accommodate the difference in teaching loads as well as performance.

Schools are explicitly required to comply with financial management guidelines and other broad city-level requirements. Schools undergo annual supervisory visits and are further subject to the comprehensive school evaluation using the "Green Indicators of Academic Quality of Primary and Secondary School Students." However, Shanghai has made a deliberate effort to not use student exam results as an explicit mechanism for rewards or sanctions. This policy seems to be directly opposite of the path taken, for example, in the United States. In fact, Shanghai uses school evaluations to identify weak and poorly performing schools and then provides additional financing and management to help those schools improve their performance. This is also contrary to what occurs in many countries, where excellent schools are identified and provided with additional rewards.

Of course in reality, the high stakes *zhong kao* at the end of ninth grade and the *gao kao* at high school graduation have tremendous downstream effects on the lower levels of education and continue to influence teaching and learning for testing purposes only. Schools continue to be assessed based on their students' performance on those tests. The government is making efforts to introduce reforms into the *gao kao* so that students have multiple chances and so that their regular grades may count in the college admission decision.

An implicit but more powerful type of professional accountability seems to be at work in Shanghai. Because principals are required to be instructional leaders, teachers are well trained and supported, and their career ladders are well established. Furthermore, because the teaching-research groups allow teachers to engage in professional development activities, professional accountability becomes more prominent.

Explicit involvement of communities and parents in the schools appears to be weak in Shanghai. By law, schools are the responsibility of their principals. Each public school is also staffed with party secretaries. In reality, the principals make most decisions in school management in consultation with party secretaries as well as the teacher and staff management committees. PTAs are set up at some schools with some limited functions. School councils are formally required for private schools but their roles and responsibilities are limited to nonteaching aspects of learning.

However, this finding also indicates that in countries where educational institutions are strong, especially in the training and selection of good teachers, autonomy and accountability in school-based management may not be a necessary condition for success. In these conditions, which are found in many high-performing countries in Europe and East Asia, trust is the main element of accountability. Parents trust and support the system because the empirical evidence—shown by the results in international testing exercises such as the Programme for International Student Assessment—indicates that it is producing good results. Nevertheless, even in high-performing countries, trust and professionalism flourish in a context of school autonomy and accountability.

References

Arcia, G., K. Macdonald, H. A. Patrinos, and E. Porta. 2011. "School Autonomy and Accountability." World Bank, Washington, DC. http://siteresources.worldbank.org /EDUCATION/Resources/278200-1290520949227/School_Autonomy_Accountability _Framework.pdf.

Demas, A., and G. Arcia. 2015. "What Matters Most for School Autonomy and Accountability: A Framework Paper." SABER Working Paper 9, World Bank, Washington, DC.

OECD (Organisation for Economic Co-operation and Development). 2013. "School Governance, Assessment and Accountability." In *What Makes Schools Successful? Resources, Policies and Practices*. Paris: OECD Publishing. http://www.oecd.org/pisa /keyfindings/Vol4Ch4.pdf.

Shanghai Municipal Education Commission. 2011. "Opinions about Further Improving the Principal Responsibility System in Primary and Secondary Schools." Shanghai. http://wenku.baidu.com/view/90fc221ba76e58fafab0030c.html?from=search.

CHAPTER 6

Creating an Effective Student Assessment System

Introduction

The student assessment module of the World Bank's Systems Approach for Better Education Results (SABER–Student Assessment) analyzes and benchmarks student assessment policies according to the available evidence base on the components and attributes of an effective assessment system. The module is structured around two main dimensions of assessment systems: the types of assessment activities that make up the system and the quality of those activities. The module aims to promote comprehensive and rigorous assessment systems that contribute to quality education.

Assessment Types and Purposes

The evidence base for this module is outlined in the 2012 SABER framework for student assessment (Clarke 2012). According to Clarke (2012, 1), *assessment* is the general process of "gathering and evaluating information about what students know, understand, and can do to make informed decisions about next steps in the educational process." Assessment systems are composed of three main types of assessment activities: classroom assessments; exams; and large-scale, system-level assessments.

- Classroom assessments (continuous or formative assessments) are carried out as part of daily classroom activities. These reviews assess ongoing teaching and learning in individual classrooms and point out areas of achievement and needed improvement. Classroom assessments encompass homework assignments, student presentations, and diagnostic quizzes and tests.
- Exams punctuate students' progression through the education system. They provide information about individual students for the purpose of selection in decision-making circumstances, such as graduation, admission, and certification.

- Large-scale, system-level assessments evaluate the performance of the overall education system and provide policy makers and practitioners with relevant information for designing and implementing education policy and practice. They may be national or international.

Three main drivers determine the effectiveness of the assessment activities in any system: the enabling context, system alignment, and assessment quality.

- *Enabling context* refers to the broader context in which the assessment activity takes place and the extent to which that context is conducive to student and teacher learning. It covers the policy framework for assessment activities; institutional structures for designing, carrying out, or using results from the assessment; the availability of sufficient and stable funding; and the presence of trained assessment staff.
- *System alignment* refers to the extent to which the assessment is aligned with the rest of the education system. This includes the degree of congruence between assessment activities and system learning goals, standards, curriculum, and pre- and in-service teacher training.
- *Assessment quality* refers to the psychometric quality of the instruments, processes, and procedures for the assessment activity. It covers design and implementation of assessment activities, analysis and interpretation of student responses to those activities, and the appropriateness of how assessment results are reported and used.

SABER–Student Assessment collects and evaluates data on the three assessment types and the related quality drivers (table 6.1). Overall, Shanghai's ratings for classroom assessments, exams, and large-scale assessment are at least "established" with some levers at the "advanced" level.

Classroom Assessments (Established)

SABER–Student Assessment indicates that classroom assessments in Shanghai are rated "established." As demonstrated in table 6.1, the three drivers of effectiveness discussed above are used to score Shanghai's achievement on classroom assessments.

Policy Goal 1: Enabling Context (Established)

Classroom assessments take place frequently in Shanghai's education system. Students participate in weekly quizzes, oral tests and presentations, and homework assignments throughout the academic year. In addition to assessments planned by teachers for each individual class of students, students in the same grade regularly participate in common weekly or monthly, midterm, or final-term paper-based assessments.

Both the central government of China and the city of Shanghai have issued formal system-level documents that provide guidelines for classroom assessment—a

Table 6.1 SABER–Student Assessment, Shanghai

Policy and resource framework (Goals and levers)	SABER score
Classroom assessments	●●●○
1. Enabling context	●●●○
2. System alignment	●●●○
3. Assessment quality	●●●○
Examinations (lower secondary graduation exam—zhong kao)	●●●○
1. Enabling context	●●●○
2. System alignment	●●●●
3. Assessment quality	●●●○
Examinations (senior secondary graduation exam—gao kao)	●●●●
1. Enabling context	●●●●
2. System alignment	●●●●
3. Assessment quality	●●●●
National assessment	●●●○
1. Enabling context	●●●○
2. System alignment	●●●○
3. Assessment quality	●●●○
International assessment	●●●○
1. Enabling context	●●●●
2. System alignment	●●●○
3. Assessment quality	●●●○

Note: Scoring rubric: Latent (●○○○), Emerging (●●○○), Established (●●●○), Advanced (●●●●).
SABER = Systems Approach for Better Education Results.

curriculum standard for each subject. The subject-specific standards include concrete knowledge areas and skills that students are expected to acquire every year (see SABER–Teachers in chapter 3). Furthermore, each set of standards includes a specific section on learning assessments. For example, for math, the national curriculum standard emphasizes that homework assignments and classroom observations should be weighted equally with quizzes and tests in evaluating student performance. Shanghai's math curriculum standard provides more detailed guidelines, identifying classroom assessments as a continuous effort to evaluate and analyze student progress throughout the learning process. The standard suggests that math assessments should focus on learning interest and attitudes, math cognitive understanding, and the ability to think analytically and innovatively in math learning. The standards encourage the use of progress indicators and include suggestions for assessment methods (such as debate, homework assignments, survey, and subject-related arts and crafts) and content. In addition, the guidelines provide information on reporting assessment results and using the results to improve individual students' performance. Both the central and municipal documents are available online for the public and teachers to review. Referencing the learning objectives listed in the curriculum standards and the guidelines on assessments, teachers are able to design effective classroom assessments.

How Shanghai Does It • http://dx.doi.org/10.1596/978-1-4648-0790-9

Policy Goal 2: System Alignment (Established)

To ensure smooth implementation of the municipal curriculum standards and the associated assessments, the Shanghai Municipal Education Commission released "Advice on Curriculum-Standards-Based Teaching and Assessments at the Primary School Level" in 2013 to instruct teachers on carrying out teaching activities and assessments in accordance with the curriculum standards. The document encourages teachers to design formative assessments that reflect students' learning outcomes and that track individual students' growth, rather than focusing on comparing students with one another. Because of the general heightened exam pressure in Shanghai, the document specifically stipulates that classroom assessments cannot take the form of paper-based tests for students in first and second grades.

In Shanghai, multiple mechanisms ensure that teachers develop the necessary skills and expertise to carry out classroom assessments. All teachers are required to participate in a one-year in-service induction program to enhance their pedagogical capacity and competence in carrying out various classroom activities, including designing classroom assessments. Furthermore, professional development activities such as teaching-research groups and lesson observations (see SABER–Teachers in chapter 3) encompass specific components that address classroom assessments, such as discussion of the design and analysis of assessments. In addition, to equip teachers with updated assessment-related knowledge and skills, the city organizes targeted training on assessments for teachers and principals. Online resources are also available for teachers planning assessment activities.

Policy Goal 3: Assessment Quality (Established)

The education system in Shanghai closely monitors classroom assessment practices. Classroom assessment is a core aspect of a teacher's performance evaluation. When a school principal or the leadership team conducts lesson observations, they closely observe the teacher's assessment activities and evaluate how the activities facilitate student learning. Classroom assessment is also a required component of school supervision by the district. To improve classroom assessment, the municipal and district-level Teaching Research Offices undertake regular research projects on the status of student assessments to inform policy decisions.

Globally, most schools use assessment data for a combination of purposes (box 6.1). In Shanghai, adequate measures are taken to ensure effective use of classroom assessments. Assessment results are recorded carefully in students' profiles and teachers' records. For schools with rigorous information systems, student data are imported into the school database. Other schools opt for paper-based systems. The assessment results are required to be disseminated to key stakeholders, including school administrators and parents. Well-equipped teachers and close monitoring contribute to high-quality classroom assessments in Shanghai. The assessments not only evaluate key

---

Box 6.1 Purposes of Student Assessment and Achievement Data

Assessment practices and purposes (OECD 2013, 148). Based on principals' responses, assessments are most commonly used in Organisation for Economic Co-operation and Development (OECD) countries to

- Inform parents about their child's progress
- Monitor the school's progress from year to year
- Identify aspects of instruction or the curriculum that could be improved
- Make decisions about whether students are held back or promoted
- Compare the school to district or national performance
- Compare the school with other schools
- Group students for instructional purposes
- Make judgments about teachers' effectiveness

The use of achievement data beyond school (OECD 2013, 152). Achievement data are used for accountability purposes involving some stakeholders beyond schools, teachers, partners, and students.

- *Posting data publicly:* On average across OECD countries, 45 percent of students are in schools whose principals reported that achievement data are posted publicly. The average is more than 80 percent in the Netherlands, New Zealand, Sweden, the United States, and the United Kingdom, and less than 10 percent in Argentina; Austria; Belgium; Finland; Japan; Macao SAR, China; Shanghai; Switzerland; and Uruguay.
- *Tracking achievement data over time:* On average across OECD countries, 72 percent of students are in schools whose principals reported that achievement data are tracked over time by an administrative authority. The average is more than 80 percent in 31 countries and economies, and 7 percent in Japan.

Source: OECD 2013.

---

knowledge areas that students are expected to acquire, but also gauge general competencies such as discipline and collaboration. The assessment results also serve to diagnose student learning issues, provide feedback to students on their learning, inform teaching, communicate with parents about their child's learning, and meet school-level requirements on assessing student achievement.

Examinations

Students take two types of exams at the municipal and national levels: (1) the citywide exam at the end of the nine-year compulsory period, which also serves as the high school entrance exam; and (2) the high school graduation exam, which also serves as the college entrance exam.

Ninth Grade Graduation or High School Entrance Exam (zhong kao)[1] (Established)

At the end of lower secondary school (ninth grade), all students must take the Lower Secondary School Graduation Examination in Shanghai. The subjects tested include Chinese, math, English, physics, and chemistry. Physical education, lab operations, and moral ethics of students also factor into students' final exam scores. The exam serves the dual purposes of selection into high schools and providing information on the overall performance of the basic education system. The total score on the exam determines the type of high school in which students will enroll: admission into highly selective comprehensive schools requires outstanding performance on the exam.

SABER–Student Assessment outlines three broad components of the policy framework (table 6.1) on which Shanghai's achievements are measured. Overall, Shanghai scores between "established" and "advanced" on the three policy goals pertaining to student assessment at the high school entrance exam level (*zhong kao*).

Policy Goal 1: Enabling Context (Established)

Formal policy documents authorize the exam. In 2014, the Shanghai Municipal Education Commission released "Advice on Lower Secondary School Graduation Examination" and "Plan on Lower Secondary School Graduation Examination." Both documents are available online. The first document announces details on the exam, including tested subjects, exam structure, scoring methods, and exemptions for students with special needs. The second document provides general guidelines on the format and scoring of the exam for each subject. Most subjects include multiple-choice questions, essay questions, or a combination of the two.

The municipal government allocates regular funding to carry out the exam, covering all aspects from design and administration to results reporting and research activities. In addition to financial support, Shanghai has a strong organizational structure and wide public support for the exam. The Shanghai Education Examination Center is the designated agency responsible for preparation and implementation of the exam. The exam is a well-recognized social event in Shanghai, closely followed by students, parents, educators, and the media. No political opposition to the exam has arisen. The Shanghai Education Examination Center is accountable to the Shanghai Municipal Education Commission.

Effective human resources are guaranteed for the exam. Not only does the Shanghai Education Examination Center have an adequate number of full-time staff dedicated to the exam, but every year the center also invites experts from across the nation to engage in its planning and design. Employees are also given opportunities to attend university courses and non-university training courses, and funding is provided for attending international programs and courses related to education measurement and evaluation.

The exam is closely aligned with the municipal curriculum standards, which include learning goals for each subject and are widely accepted by stakeholder groups.

Policy Goal 2: System Alignment (Advanced)

Teachers are provided with information and training opportunities with regard to the exam. Based on the 2009 "Advice on Designing Lower Secondary School Graduation Examination in Shanghai," a systematic method is in place for selecting and organizing teachers for the design and scoring of the exam. The teacher candidates must have substantial teaching experience, and must be recommended by the district Department of Education for involvement in either the design or the scoring process. The document stipulates that at least one-third of the personnel must change every year, and recommends a maximum three-year tenure. The city also organizes systematic training for those teachers, specially targeted at equipping them with the competence to conduct exam-related work.

Shanghai has taken some measures to ensure the fairness and quality of the exam. At the policy level, special accommodations are provided for students with hearing disabilities, and they are exempt from the listening component of the English subject test. It might be desirable to stipulate recommendations or alternative assessments for students with other types of disabilities.

Policy Goal 3: Assessment Quality (Established)

Because of its primary purpose as a mechanism for selection into high school, the *zhong kao* has become increasingly high stakes for children in Shanghai. The test ultimately determines in which type of high school ninth-grade graduates can enroll. There are three types of high schools in Shanghai: ordinary general high school, model or experimental general high school, and vocational high school. Each type of school has a minimum score entry requirement. Model or experimental high schools have the highest required entry score and vocational high schools the lowest (or no requirement in some schools) (table 6.2).

As can easily be imagined, the model and experimental senior secondary schools are able to enroll the best graduates and cumulatively attract more highly qualified and experienced teachers and create a virtuous cycle of "good students– good teachers–excellent schools–and more good students." Model and experimental senior secondary schools are highly sought after by both parents and children. These schools also send more of their graduates to the best universities and colleges in China and worldwide. In contrast, vocational senior secondary schools tend to enroll predominantly low-performing students. Although recent government efforts to revive vocational education and boost the employment rates of vocational school graduates are indeed promising, stigma continues to be associated with vocational education and it is a second choice for most graduates.

Table 6.2 *Zhong Kao* Entry Score Requirement in 2015

Type of senior secondary school	Zhong kao *entry score*
Model or experimental senior secondary school	555
Ordinary senior secondary school	475
Vocational senior secondary school	330

Source: Shanghai Municipal Education Commission, 2015, http://www.shanghai.gov.cn/.

Coordinated efforts are ongoing to reform the exam to reduce pressure on families and students. The format of the various subject exams have undergone a number of rounds of change. Physical education was added to the exam in 2008 to encourage students to be more physically active. Furthermore, in response to the recent *gao kao* reform pilot in Shanghai, the city is planning to reform the Lower Secondary Graduation Examination in 2016.

Twelfth Grade Graduation or College Entrance Exam (gao kao) (Advanced)

Students in Shanghai participate in the national college entrance exams (*gao kao*). *Gao kao* is a highly competitive and rigorous exam that students across the nation have to take at the end of high school (twelfth grade) to progress to tertiary education in China. Students sit for the three-day exam during June. It has been administered on a yearly basis since 1977. The exam is mostly paper based, plus a physical exam. The tested subjects vary by region, but they commonly include Chinese, math, English, and a subject in the humanities or sciences chosen by the student. Although provinces can choose to use the national version of the exam questions, many provinces and cities opt to develop their own questions, which conform to national guidelines. Depending on the subject, exam questions can be multiple choice questions, open-ended questions, and essays. Whether a student can attend university and which tier of university depends almost exclusively on the exam score.

Most Chinese people would agree that the high-stakes *gao kao* has taken on special significance in Chinese society. As with *zhong kao*, *gao kao* results determine not only whether a student is eligible for college but also which type of college. Chinese universities are ranked and grouped into four tiers: The first-tier universities, consisting of the elite Chinese universities, mostly centrally managed, aim at producing the best talent in various fields. The second-tier universities are mainly provincial or city-level universities that aim at producing professional-level skills. The third tier universities mainly comprise private colleges; and the least attractive, tier four, are diploma-granting technical and vocational colleges, which aim at producing skills. The Ministry of Education announces cutoff scores for each tier after the exam (table 6.3). Only those with a score higher than the cutoff score for the particular tier are eligible for enrollment in the associated universities.

Policy Goal 1: Enabling Context (Advanced)

The national policies on *gao kao* are clear. Every year, the Ministry of Education releases a public document authorizing the implementation of *gao kao*. The 2014 "Regulations on Tertiary Institutions Admission" provides detailed information on all key aspects of the 2014 *gao kao* process. According to the document, the Ministry of Education is the primary body responsible for coordinating *gao kao*, with key participation from the National Examination Center, provincial *gao kao* committees, and relevant tertiary institutions. Not only does the document cover the *gao kao*'s purpose and governance structure, exam registration requirements, and collection of student data, it also provides comprehensive regulations on

Table 6.3 *Gao Kao* **Minimum Entry Score Requirement in 2015 and 2014, Shanghai**

Type of college		Gao kao *entry score (2015)*	Gao kao *entry score (2014)*
Tier 1: Elite universities	Liberal arts majors	434	448
	Science majors	414	405
Tier 2: Ordinary universities	Liberal arts majors	372	403
	Science majors	348	331
Tier 3: Private colleges	Liberal arts majors	—[a]	—[a]
	Science majors	—[a]	—[a]
Tier 4: Technical and vocational education colleges	Liberal arts majors	144[b]	108[b]
	Science majors	194[b]	158[b]

Source: Gao Kao Inquiry System. 2015. "*Gao Kao* Minimum Entry Score Requirement." http://www.eol.cn/html/g/fsx/gedi/shanghai.shtml.
a. Scores may vary significantly from college to college. Aggregate or ranges of scores are not available.
b. Combined score on three subjects—Chinese, math, and English. Other scores are combined scores on five or six subjects.

implementation, including how to address inappropriate behaviors in the exams (such as cheating, bribing, and leaking exam questions), procedures for students with special needs, and the selection and admission process for entry into tertiary institutions.

Fairly strong leadership is in place for the preparation and implementation of *gao kao*. The Ministry of Education delegates primary responsibility for the design of the exam questions and the scoring rubric to the National Examination Center, provincial *gao kao* committees, and relevant tertiary institutions. The National Examination Center takes the lead in designing the national *gao kao*, while province-specific *gao kao* questions are developed by provincial-level *gao kao* committees. A number of elite universities in China are also granted permission to develop their own entrance exam questions for the exclusive use of their own admission processes.

The primary stakeholder groups for the exam include students, universities, and high schools, and they have provided continuous support for the exam. The results of the exam are acknowledged nationally and used as a primary indicator of college admission. *Gao kao* is also a well-recognized social event in Chinese society, garnering wide media coverage around the time the exam is administered. Local governments across the country coordinate special traffic and security measures to facilitate students' attendance in the exam.

Funding for *gao kao* preparation and implementation is a regular component of local education expenditure under the 2014 "Regulations on Tertiary Institutions Admission." Students participating in *gao kao* also must pay a fee. Funding covers all core exam activities, including design of the exam, administration, data analysis, reporting, and research and development.

Behind the planning and implementation of *gao kao* is a strong organizational structure. The Ministry of Education steers the process. The ministry sets overall policy, reviews provincial exam plans, authorizes the design of exam questions, and monitors implementation. The National Examination Center and provincial *gao kao* committees take the lead in the design of exam questions, scoring, and data analysis. The provincial *gao kao* committees are also responsible for organizing administration of the exam. This sound institutional structure ensures that staff and resources are adequate to execute *gao kao* smoothly every year.

Policy Goal 2: System Alignment (Advanced)

The exam is in accordance with national curriculum guidelines and standards. Because the exam questions vary by region, they also reflect regional curriculum standards, which are widely accepted by all stakeholder groups. Students undergo intensive preparation for *gao kao*, dedicating the last year of high school almost exclusively to demanding school drills, practice tests, and after-school tutoring sessions. In some regions, *gao kao* preparation starts on the first day of high school. Comprehensive material is available to prepare for the exam. Each school provides students with learning material, and various publications with practice tests are on the market. Preparation also references past *gao kao* questions and a framework document explaining what is measured on the exam. Teachers play an important role in *gao kao*; they are involved in creating and selecting exam questions, as well as participating in administering, scoring, and supervising the exam.

Policy Goal 3: Assessment Quality (Advanced)

To ensure that the assessment meets quality standards and is carried out effectively, the "Regulations on Tertiary Institutions Admission" serves as a comprehensive technical report, and is available to the general public. The *gao kao* undergoes a rigorous quality assurance procedure, including internal and external review, external certification, piloting, and translation verification. The processes and results of the exam are closely monitored by mechanisms such as an oversight committee and expert review groups.

All students with a senior secondary or equivalent education are eligible to take the exam. Various measures are taken to ensure that *gao kao* is fair. Inappropriate behavior is strictly forbidden in the exam process and such incidents are rare. To ensure the security of the exam questions, they are stored in a room with a closed iron gate, five security cameras, and 24-hour supervision. If instances of impersonation, copying, collusion among candidates, and cheating occur, the exam results are deemed invalid. With strict monitoring, *gao kao* results are widely accepted by all stakeholder groups.

Students' test results are confidential. The results are used primarily for selection into tertiary institutions. One common criticism of the *gao kao* is that it gives students only one chance at the end of their 12-year education to enter a university. If a student receives a low score, he or she must study for another year to prepare for the exam. Students also have the option of attending less selective schools that match their *gao kao* scores.

The government has set a 1:1 ratio between enrollment in degree programs and enrollment in diploma programs. Entry scores are centrally determined, with research universities (tier one) having the highest entry requirement and the technical and vocational colleges having the lowest requirements. Therefore, even when Shanghai tries to ease the exam pressure felt by students in basic education, the prospect of participating in *gao kao* inevitably poses a burden on students, who undertake intensive exam-preparation drills throughout their education before attending university, particularly during the high school years.

The one-child policy introduced in the late 1970s means that most Chinese families today have a single child who increasingly must shoulder the high expectations of two parents and four grandparents. Students in Shanghai are found to have one of the heaviest homework loads as revealed by the student questionnaire on the Programme for International Student Assessment (PISA) tests, with about 11 hours per week devoted to homework.

The overemphasis on exam scores has drawn increasing criticism because of the tremendous pressure it imposes on students and incentives teachers have to teach to the test while overlooking students' overall development. In response, the Chinese State Council released a plan in September 2014 to overhaul the college entrance exam and enrollment system by 2020. The reform involves major changes to the current *gao kao* system: the final exam score includes results on Chinese, math, and English tests at the end of high school and three self-selected subject tests taken throughout high school; students also have two chances in the same year to take the English test. The reform is being piloted in Shanghai and Zhejiang Province and started with the 2014 high school freshman cohort. The pilot experience will be summarized and expanded in 2017. By 2020, a new recruiting and enrollment system will be established and promoted nationwide.

National Large-Scale Assessment (Established)

As part of the government's efforts to monitor the quality of basic education and in particular to improve the quality of education in rural and less developed areas, China began piloting a national assessment in 2008. During a seven-year piloting stage the government developed the testing instruments, piloted them in selected schools and counties, and established relevant institutions at national, provincial, and county education offices. The State Council formally rolled out the Plan for National Compulsory Education Quality Monitoring in April 2015. The plan outlines an annual sample-based assessment in two subject areas for fourth- and eighth-grade students, thus covering six main subject areas (Chinese, mathematics, science, physical education, art, and moral education) within a three-year period.

The first assessment in math and physical education was completed in June 2015 covering a total of 200,000 students in fourth and eighth grades in 6,476 primary and lower secondary schools in 323 counties and 31 provinces throughout China. In addition, about 6,500 principals and 100,000 teachers of math and physical education provided feedback through structured questionnaires.[2]

In 2011, the Shanghai Municipal Educational Commission launched a series of surveys entitled "Green Indicators of Academic Quality of Primary and

Secondary School Students." The general aims of these surveys are to satisfy the requirements for connotative development in the educational domain, optimize educational management, and build a fine educational ecology. Generally, the indicators in these surveys include student academic achievement, student learning motivation, student academic workload, teacher-student relations, teachers' instructional styles, principals' curriculum leadership, the impact of students' socioeconomic background on their academic achievement, students' moral behavior, and annual progress on these indicators. The potential participants for these surveys include all primary and junior secondary students in the compulsory education stage. For 2011, the sampled students were those in fourth and ninth grades. The survey instruments included academic tests (Chinese language and math for primary students and Chinese language, math, foreign language, and sciences for junior secondary students), questionnaires (for students, teachers, and principals), and student physical health monitoring.

International Large-Scale Assessment (Established)

Shanghai is one of the pioneer Chinese cities in participating in international assessments. In both 2009 and 2012, the city participated in the PISA. The city has also announced plans to participate in PISA 2015, along with a number Chinese cities and provinces that will be participating for the first time.

Overall, based on SABER–Student Assessment indicators for these goals, Shanghai is rated between "advanced" and "established." Although Shanghai's performance on PISA has been outstanding, with its cutting-edge provisions for ensuring an enabling environment for conducting international evaluation, its performance with regard to professional development of teachers on PISA and postevaluation use of the assessment data is rated "established," not "advanced."

Policy Goal 1: Enabling Context (Advanced)

For both PISA 2009 and 2012, the Shanghai Municipal Education Commission released an announcement informing the public of the city's participation in the assessment and seeking the collaboration of all relevant entities in the organization and implementation. The financial allocation for PISA participation came from the commission's regular research funding, covering all core activities including participation, implementation, data processing and analysis, and research and dissemination of results.

To facilitate the PISA process, Shanghai designed a comprehensive management system. For assessment activities on the ground, the city established the Shanghai PISA Committee (SHPISA) in 2007 to be in charge of assessment implementation and research activities and a Shanghai PISA coordinator was appointed. The coordinator was an expert in Shanghai's education system and then president of a local university. For municipal-level coordination and advising, the Shanghai Municipal Education Commission established a steering committee comprising four relevant offices under the commission: the examination center, SHPISA, the municipal education research center, and the municipal education evaluation center. The committee also invited experts to provide advice and suggestions on assessment implementation. This fully staffed PISA team not only encompassed experience and expertise to carry out the assessment activities effectively and accurately, it also ensured cross-departmental coordination and wide dissemination of PISA results. As a result, both rounds of PISA took place smoothly and without error in Shanghai.

Policy Goal 2: System Alignment (Established)

Shanghai offered a number of opportunities for citizens and students to learn about PISA, including workshops, university courses, and funding for attending workshops. Individuals working in the field, university students studying the topic, and professionals interested in assessment all benefited from those opportunities.

Policy Goal 3: Assessment Quality (Established)

Shanghai met all technical standards required to have its data included in the main portion of the Organisation for Economic Co-operation and Development (OECD) PISA report. The results were also publicized domestically. A number of major Chinese newspapers reported the results on the front page on the day the results were released. Extensive media coverage and discussion followed in the succeeding months. The results for individual participating schools, however, were not made available to schools to avoid academic pressure and competition given that the city views the assessment as a diagnostic tool for the entire education system rather than an evaluation of individual schools.

For both 2009 and 2012, Shanghai was the top performer among all the participating countries and regions, and its performance attracted international attention. In the OECD's PISA publication *Strong Performers and Successful Reformers in Education: Lessons from PISA for the United States* (OECD 2011), Shanghai's education system is featured in chapter 4, "Shanghai and Hong Kong: Two Distinct Examples of Education Reform in China." Various media sources such as the *New York Times* and the BBC have published articles analyzing Shanghai's education policies in light of the assessment results. The wide dissemination of Shanghai's PISA results has contributed to the global knowledge base on international assessments and education reform. Shanghai has also received visits from a number of countries including the United States, the United Kingdom, and Australia to share the characteristics of its education system. In November 2015, the United Kingdom entered a Math Teacher Exchange Program to offer bilateral pedagogy and exchange of learning ideas between Shanghai and the United Kingdom.

The PISA results have a significant impact on decision making at the policy level. Chinese education researchers have conducted in-depth analyses of Shanghai's PISA performance to determine strengths and weaknesses. Furthermore, the city organized a number of workshops and seminars discussing the results with key stakeholders. Because PISA offers comprehensive data on student background, teachers, and students' analytical skills, the results are used to improve the quality of the curriculum, teacher training, assessment, and resource allocation at the system level. The results informed the design of the basic education section of Shanghai's "Medium- and Long-Term Education Reform and Development Plan Outline (2010–2020)," a key policy document for Shanghai's education development.

Summary

The application of SABER–Assessment provides a comprehensive picture of student assessment in Shanghai, ranging from ongoing classroom assessment to citywide and nationwide exams, and further to large-scale national and international assessments. Again, careful benchmarking indicates that Shanghai falls in at least the "established" category and some aspects are in the "advanced" category.

China has a long tradition of exams. The imperial examination, a civil service examination system in Imperial China, was used to select candidates for the state bureaucracy as early as AD 600 in the Tang dynasty. Student exams today are still influenced by this tradition, and selection continues to be the predominant purpose of exams. After a temporary disruption during the Cultural Revolution from 1966 to about 1976, student assessment in China has evolved into a complex multilevel system, with both high-stakes selection tests, diagnostic classroom tests, and large-scale sample-based assessments.

Because of high-quality teacher training and the teaching-research group structure that fosters ongoing professional development of teachers, including in student assessment, China and Shanghai are particularly strong with regard to classroom assessment, which is closely linked to ongoing teaching and learning improvements at the school level.

Although the government has made significant efforts at the policy level to reduce the burden on students by discouraging testing during the compulsory period, the *gao kao* and *zhong kao* undoubtedly have cast a ripple effect onto the system as early as preprimary education. It remains a priority for the government to continue to reform the *zhong kao* and *gao kao* to reduce its overwhelming importance by increasing the frequency of tests, broadening the areas of testing, and creating multiple pathways between types and levels of education to alleviate the fear that parents and children have that once they fail the tests, there will not be another chance. Shanghai is currently piloting *gao kao* and *zhong kao* reform and will roll out a revised and more flexible format in 2017–18.

Future efforts can be directed more toward further development of large-scale and sample-based diagnostic tests. China first implemented the national assessment of basic education quality in 2015. There is a tremendous opportunity to build capacity to further improve the assessment and use the results effectively for policy making, in particular to reduce the vast quality gaps between provinces and between rural and urban counties, and between poor and rich areas. More Chinese provinces should also be encouraged and provided with incentives to partake in international assessments so that a China-wide picture of education quality can be revealed. Shanghai was the only mainland Chinese "province" that participated in PISA in 2009 and 2012. In 2015, however, a few more Chinese provinces participated.

Finally, China has a strong tradition and capacity for developing and implementing tests. Although cognitive tests have been dominant, more effort can be devoted to assessing students social-emotional and other skills that may be relevant for the labor market of the future.

Notes

1. Before 2005, graduates from the ninth grade of basic education had to take two types of exam: one graduation test to demonstrate proficiency and eligibility for a certificate, another solely for selection into high schools. The two tests were merged into one test serving both purposes in 2005.

2. Ministry of Education of the People's Republic of China 2015. "National Compulsory Education Quality Monitoring Smoothly Completed" (http://www.moe.edu.cn/jyb _xwfb/gzdt_gzdt/moe_1485/201506/t20150629_191522.html).

References

Clarke, Marguerite. 2012. "What Matters Most for Student Assessment Systems: A Framework Paper." SABER Working Paper, World Bank, Washington, DC. https:// openknowledge.worldbank.org/bitstream/handle/10986/17471/682350WP00PUBL 0WP10READ0web04019012.pdf?sequence=1.

OECD (Organisation for Economic Co-operation and Development). 2011. *Strong Performers and Successful Reformers in Education: Lessons from PISA for the United States*. Paris: OECD Publishing.

——— 2013. "School Governance, Assessment and Accountability." In *What Makes Schools Successful? Resources, Policies and Practices*. Paris: OECD Publishing. http:// www.oecd.org/pisa/keyfindings/Vol4Ch4.pdf.

CHAPTER 7

Linking Policies and Implementation to Learning Outcomes

Introduction

This chapter focuses on analyzing student learning outcomes in Shanghai and examines how varying characteristics and education practices across schools are correlated with student learning outcomes, as measured by the 2012 Programme for International Student Assessment (PISA) results. PISA is designed to measure the cognitive skills of 15-year-olds, mainly in math, science, and reading. The 2012 PISA also included for the first time a module on "problem-solving skills," which is paid particular attention to in this chapter (box 7.1).

Shanghai's Performance on PISA 2012

A total of 5,177 students from 155 schools in Shanghai participated in PISA 2012 (tables 7.1 and 7.2). Sampling was done in strict accordance with Organisation for Economic Co-operation and Development (OECD) protocol and quality assurance to generate a representative sample of 15-year-olds in school in Shanghai.

Shanghai continued to be the top performer on all three major domains of PISA (mathematics, reading, and science) in 2012. Its mean mathematics score of 613 points, representing a 4.2 percent annualized increase from 2009, is 119 points above the OECD average, the equivalent of nearly three years of schooling. Its mean score of 570 points in reading represents an annualized improvement of 4.6 percent since 2009 and is equivalent to more than a year and a half of schooling above the OECD average of 496 points. Its mean score in science, 580, is more than three-quarters of a proficiency level above the OECD average of 501 points.

Furthermore, Shanghai also had the largest proportion of top performers (proficient at level 5 or 6) in mathematics (55.4 percent), reading (25.1 percent), and science (27.2 percent). Particularly, with 30.8 percent of students attaining level 6 in mathematics, Shanghai is the only PISA participant with more students

Box 7.1 Definitions of PISA Domains

Reading literacy: An individual's capacity to understand, use, reflect on, and engage with written texts, so as to achieve one's goals, to develop one's knowledge and potential, and to participate in society.

Mathematical literacy: An individual's capacity to identify and understand the role that mathematics plays in the world, to make well-founded judgments, and to use and engage with mathematics in ways that meet the needs of that individual's life as a constructive, concerned, and reflective citizen.

Scientific literacy: An individual's scientific knowledge and use of that knowledge to identify questions, to acquire new knowledge, to explain scientific phenomena, and to draw evidence-based conclusions about science-related issues; understanding of the characteristic features of science as a form of human knowledge and enquiry; awareness of how science and technology shape our material, intellectual, and cultural environments; and willingness to engage in science-related issues, and with the ideas of science, as a reflective citizen.

Problem-solving skills: The problem-solving assessment of PISA 2012 was designed to focus as much as possible on cognitive processes and generic skills rather than domain-specific knowledge. Problem-solving competence is defined as an individual's capacity to engage in cognitive processing to understand and resolve problem situations where a method of solution is not immediately obvious. It includes the willingness to engage with such situations to achieve one's potential as a constructive and reflective citizen.

Source: OECD 2013, 4, 17.

Table 7.1 Number of Schools in PISA 2012 Shanghai Sample

Type of school	Number of schools
Junior secondary school	60
Mixed senior secondary school	23
General senior secondary school	40
Model or experimental	*21*
Ordinary	*19*
Vocational secondary school	32
Total	**155**

Source: Data from OECD 2012, PISA 2012 database (http://pisa2012.acer.edu.au/).
Note: PISA = Programme for International Student Assessment.

at this top level than at any other level. Moreover, Shanghai is one of the most equal education systems among the PISA participants. For example, it has the highest proportion of resilient students (19.2 percent), that is, disadvantaged students who perform among the top 25 percent of students across all participating countries and economies after controlling for socioeconomic status. The strength of the relationship between mathematics performance and socioeconomic status is also below the OECD average.

Table 7.2 Number of Students in PISA 2012 Shanghai Sample, by Type of School and Program

Program	Type of school	Number of students
Junior secondary/general	Junior secondary school	1,899
	Mixed senior secondary school	433
	General senior secondary school	31[a]
Senior secondary/general	General	1,381
	Vocational	4[a]
	Mixed	346
Senior secondary/vocational	Vocational secondary school	1,083
Total		**5,177**

Source: Data from OECD 2012, PISA 2012 database (http://pisa2012.acer.edu.au/).
Note: PISA = Programme for International Student Assessment.
a. These students attend a general junior secondary program in a general secondary school, or they attend a general senior secondary program in a vocational secondary school.

Table 7.3 Performance on Mathematics, Science, Reading, and Problem Solving, by Program and Ordinary versus Model

PISA scores

Subject	Junior secondary	Senior secondary general	Senior secondary vocational	Ordinary	Model	Shanghai
Mathematics	592	684	540	662	718	613
S.E.	6.27	3.71	4.78	5.79	6.26	3.29
Science	566	636	520	625	657	580
S.E.	5.69	3.12	4.15	3.81	5.56	3.03
Reading	554	623	515	608	649	570
S.E.	5.49	3.08	3.95	3.05	5.44	2.86
Problem solving	514	593	493	578	616	536
S.E.	6.01	4.33	4.83	6.93	7.06	3.29

Source: Data from OECD 2012, PISA 2012 database (http://pisa2012.acer.edu.au/).
Note: PISA = Programme for International Student Assessment; S.E. = standard error.

Comparing Performance between Programs

Among 15-year-olds in Shanghai, students attending senior secondary general programs achieved the highest scores on all four PISA domains (mathematics, science, reading, and problem solving), followed by those attending junior secondary programs (table 7.3).

The gap between general and vocational senior secondary students is particularly large. In fact, the average scores of vocational senior secondary students are lower than those of general junior secondary students on all four domains (figure 7.1).

Among senior secondary general program students, those attending model or experimental schools scored higher than those attending ordinary schools on all four domains. If model or experimental school students are compared with vocational school students, the largest gap in performances is 178 points (on mathematics).

Figure 7.1 Performance on Mathematics, Science, Reading, and Problem Solving, by Program and Ordinary versus Model

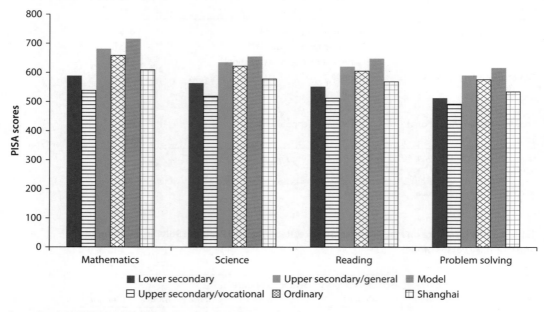

Source: Data from OECD 2012, PISA 2012 database (http://pisa2012.acer.edu.au/).
Note: PISA = Programme for International Student Assessment.

Comparative data from the 2012 OECD report reveal that between-school variation explains 47 percent of the total variation in mathematics performance among students in Shanghai for PISA 2012, slightly higher than Hong Kong SAR, China (40 percent); Taiwan, China (40 percent); the Republic of Korea (39 percent); and Singapore (37 percent); but lower than Japan (53 percent) (figure 7.2).

Additionally, it was found that as much as 58.8 percent of the between-school difference in Shanghai is explained by study programs (lower vs. upper level and vocational vs. general orientation), much higher than the OECD average (40 percent) and other education systems in the region (for example, 7.6 percent in Hong Kong SAR, China; 13 percent in Japan; and 35 percent in Korea and Taiwan, China).

The following sections first compare the student and school characteristics between programs, then investigate, within each program (junior secondary, senior secondary general, and senior secondary vocational), how school-level characteristics are associated with student performance.

Comparing Individual and Family Background Characteristics between Programs

Individual and family characteristics of students attending junior secondary, general senior secondary, and vocational senior secondary programs differ significantly from each other (table 7.4). A total of 56 percent of general senior secondary

Figure 7.2 Percentage of Total Variation in PISA Mathematics Performance Explained by Between-School Variation and Study Programs (junior or senior secondary level, vocational or general)

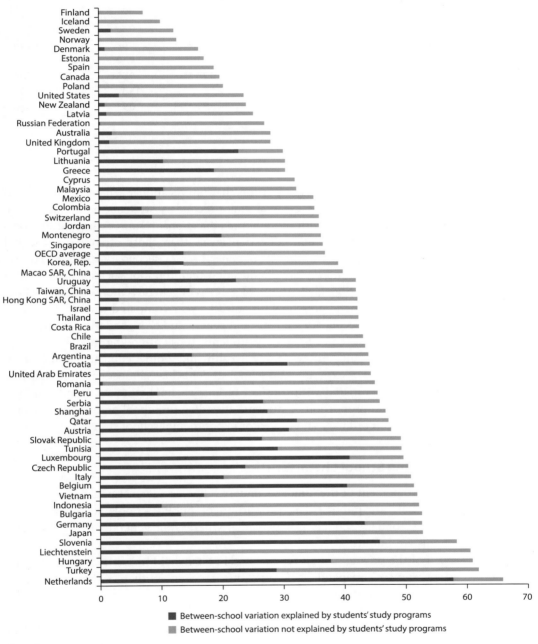

■ Between-school variation explained by students' study programs

▨ Between-school variation not explained by students' study programs

Source: Data from OECD 2012, PISA 2012 database (http://pisa2012.acer.edu.au/).

Note: OECD = Organisation for Economic Co-operation and Development; PISA = Programme for International Student Assessment.

Table 7.4 Comparing Individual and Family Characteristics by Program

PISA variable	Junior secondary	Senior secondary general	Senior secondary vocational	Ordinary	Model	All programs
female	0.48	0.56	0.51***	0.56	0.58	0.51
WEALTH	−0.87	−0.53	−0.91***	−0.62	−0.47*	−0.76
HEDRES	−0.15	0.20	−0.14***	0.10	0.29*	−0.03
CULTPOS	0.41	0.68	0.22***	0.65	0.73	0.46
PARED	12.46	13.80	11.89***	13.31	14.30***	12.79
preschool	0.85	0.93	0.85***	0.93	0.93	0.88

Source: Data from OECD 2012, PISA 2012 database (http://pisa2012.acer.edu.au/).
Note: See variable descriptions in table 7A.1. PISA = Programme for International Student Assessment.
*$p < 0.05$, **$p < 0.01$, ***$p < 0.001$.

students are girls, a higher proportion than in vocational senior secondary and junior secondary programs. General senior secondary students, on average, come from wealthier families with more home educational resources and cultural possessions and higher parental education levels than those attending vocational senior secondary programs. Parents of general senior secondary students have on average almost two more years of education than those of vocational senior secondary students in Shanghai. About 93 percent of general senior secondary school students have attended preschool for at least a year, compared with 85 percent of vocational senior secondary students and general junior secondary students.

Among general senior secondary students, those attending model or experimental schools enjoy more family wealth and home educational resources. Parents of model or experimental school students have almost an additional year of education compared with those of ordinary school students. Family cultural possessions and proportion of students attending preschool do not differ significantly between ordinary and model or experimental school students.

Comparing School Characteristics

About 90 percent of the junior secondary schools and vocational senior secondary schools are public.[1] The proportion of public schools is lowest among mixed secondary schools (76 percent), whereas all general senior secondary schools are public.

All of the private schools represented in Shanghai PISA 2012 are categorized as government-independent because they receive less than 50 percent of their core funding from the government. Among the private school student population in Shanghai, 36 percent attend private schools with no funding from the government; an equal percentage attend schools that rely completely on student fees. Half of private school students attend schools that receive about 10–30 percent of funding from government; 5.8 percent attend schools that receive approximately 45 percent of their core funding from the government. In contrast, funding sources seem to vary among public schools: among public school students in Shanghai, only 60 percent attend schools that do not charge

Figure 7.3 Distribution of Students by Percentage of Funding from Government versus Student Fees

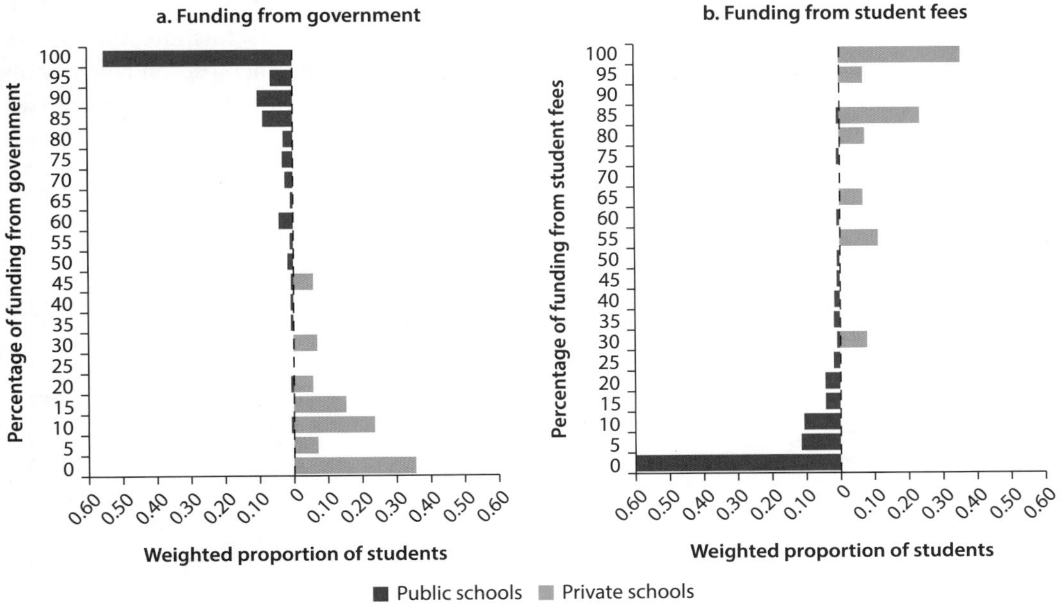

a. Funding from government

b. Funding from student fees

Weighted proportion of students

Weighted proportion of students

■ Public schools ■ Private schools

Source: Data from OECD 2012, PISA 2012 database (http://pisa2012.acer.edu.au/).

student fees as a funding source. As shown in figure 7.3, panel a, a small proportion of public schools in Shanghai actually receive less than half of their core funding from the government. And 3 percent of the public school student population in Shanghai in fact attends public schools that receive more than half of their core funding from student fees (figure 7.3, panel b).

Admissions policies differ significantly among the four types of schools: 17 percent of junior secondary schools still consider academic performance or recommendations from feeder schools for admission. Academic performance or recommendations from feeder schools is required for admission to the vast majority (92 percent) of general secondary schools, but only for 60 percent of vocational secondary schools. This means that the variation in student performance across and within senior secondary programs is not only related to school quality, but also to the admission process that sorts students according to their academic performance before they enter senior secondary school. Considering that the PISA was administered not long after the 15-year-olds entered senior secondary programs, the correlations presented in the following sections can be interpreted both as "what school characteristics predict better student performance" and as "what kinds of schools attract better-performing students?"

The main difference between general and vocational secondary schools lies in teaching resources: the student-to-teacher ratio is as high as 17 in vocational secondary schools, in contrast with 9 in general secondary schools. Moreover, on average 99 percent of the teachers in general senior secondary schools hold tertiary qualifications, compared with 92 percent in vocational senior secondary schools. In addition, more creative extracurricular activities are available at senior secondary schools and mixed secondary schools than at junior secondary schools.

Curiously, measures of student- and teacher-related factors affecting school climate are lowest in vocational schools but highest in general secondary schools (table 7.5). Given that both measures are based on principals' reporting (see table 7A.1 for detailed definitions of the two measures), it is likely that, instead

Table 7.5 Comparing Characteristics of Different Types of Schools

PISA variable	Junior secondary school	Mixed secondary	General high	Vocational high	Total
Organization, competition, and policy					
public	0.90	0.76	1.00	0.91***	0.91
compete	0.73	0.89	0.86	0.87	0.82
academic	0.17	0.61	0.92	0.60***	0.53
abg_math	0.95	0.95	0.92	0.93	0.94
Teacher					
STRATIO	11.52	11.61	9.27	17.23***	12.22
PROPQUAL	0.93	0.96	0.99	0.92***	0.95
TCMORALE	0.10	−0.01	0.01	−0.35	−0.04
Shortage_scie	0.38	0.37	0.25	0.45	0.36
Shortage_math	0.36	0.46	0.27	0.42	0.36
Shortage_read	0.33	0.42	0.27	0.32	0.32
Resources					
SCMATEDU	0.22	0.01	0.34	−0.10	0.15
SCMATBUI	−0.18	−0.39	0.10	−0.19	−0.14
COMPWEB	0.98	0.96	0.99	0.86	0.95
CLSIZE	38.63	39.23	38.11	41.59	39.25
CREACTIV	1.74	2.55	2.76	2.46***	2.30
Autonomy					
RESPRES	−0.29	−0.28	−0.46	−0.03	−0.27
RESPCUR	−0.71	−0.87	−0.77	0.29	−0.52
Accountability					
Ppressure	0.20	0.39	0.17	0.10	0.19
scoretrack	0.68	0.81	0.57	0.41	0.61
Climate					
STUDCLIM	0.53	−0.08	0.89	−1.06	0.18
TEACCLIM	−0.61	−1.00	−0.23	−1.16	−0.69
Leadership					
LEADCOM	−0.32	−0.32	−0.26	−0.69	−0.39
LEADINST	−0.13	−0.11	−0.24	−0.44	−0.23
LEADPD	−0.08	−0.33	−0.29	−0.54	−0.28
LEADTCH	−0.80	−0.71	−0.81	−0.87	−0.80

Source: Data from OECD 2012, PISA 2012 database (http://pisa2012.acer.edu.au/).
Note: See variable descriptions in table 7A.1. PISA = Programme for International Student Assessment.
*$p < 0.05$, **$p < 0.01$, ***$p < 0.001$.

of measuring the actual extent of disruption, the two variables indicate how aware principals are of disruptive student behaviors and teaching practices. Thus, caution should be exercised in interpreting these results.

Among general secondary schools, the only statistically significant difference between ordinary and model or experimental schools lies in the student-to-teacher ratio and class sizes (table 7.6): model or experimental schools have relatively

Table 7.6 Comparing Characteristics of Ordinary versus Model or Experimental Secondary Schools

PISA variable	Ordinary	Model or experimental
Organization, competition, and policy		
public	1.00	1.00
compete	0.83	0.89
academic	0.94	0.90
abg_math	0.94	0.89
Teacher		
STRATIO	8.80	9.71*
PROPQUAL	1.00	0.99
TCMORALE	−0.11	0.14
Shortage_scie	0.23	0.26
Shortage_math	0.35	0.21
Shortage_read	0.28	0.26
Resources		
SCMATEDU	0.25	0.44
SCMATBUI	−0.11	0.30
COMPWEB	0.99	0.98
CLSIZE	35.25	40.87***
CREACTIV	2.62	2.89
Autonomy		
RESPRES	−0.52	−0.41
RESPCUR	−0.90	−0.66
Accountability		
Ppressure	0.17	0.16
scoretrack	0.57	0.58
Climate		
STUDCLIM	0.47	1.30
TEACCLIM	−0.15	−0.31
Leadership		
LEADCOM	−0.32	−0.20
LEADINST	−0.31	−0.17
LEADPD	−0.36	−0.23
LEADTCH	−0.99	−0.63

Source: Data from OECD 2012, PISA 2012 database (http://pisa2012.acer.edu.au/).
Note: See variable descriptions in table 7A.1. PISA = Programme for International Student Assessment.
*$p < 0.05$, ** $p < 0.01$, *** $p < 0.001$.

higher student-to-teacher ratios (10) and larger class sizes (41) than ordinary secondary schools. The greater local demand for model schools in general perhaps explains these differences. This variation also seems to indicate that smaller class size and student-to-teacher ratios themselves do not automatically translate to learning achievement. Model or experimental school principals reported higher levels of student-related factors that affect school climate, suggesting that they might be more aware of student disruptive behaviors.

Estimating Mathematical, Reading, and Scientific Literacy

How are different school characteristics associated with students' mathematical, reading, and scientific literacy? For each program (junior secondary, senior secondary general, and senior secondary vocational), PISA scores are estimated on the three domains (mathematics, science, and reading) using school characteristics, controlling for individual and family background characteristics. Given that students were sorted into general versus vocational programs through *zhong kao* at the end of ninth grade and not long before PISA was administered, separate regression models for each program are estimated (junior secondary, senior secondary general, and senior secondary vocational). In interpreting the results, we do not intend to draw any causal inferences from the estimates; rather, we aim to characterize schools with better- versus worse-performing students. We also emphasize that the relationship can be interpreted both ways: better-quality schools produce better student performance, but they also admit better-performing students to start with.

Junior Secondary

After controlling for student and family background characteristics, differences in junior secondary students' mathematics, reading, and science scores are associated mainly with public vs. private administration of the junior secondary schools: private junior secondary school students, on average, perform better than public school students on all three domains, and the differences are statistically significant for mathematics and reading scores.

Measures of teachers and teaching resources do not seem to explain variances in junior secondary school student performance except that better-performing schools on the reading test are more likely to report shortages of teachers of Chinese. Among indicators of school resources, creative extracurricular activities available at school are related to better performances of students across all three domains.

Lower-performing junior secondary schools tend to be more autonomous in determining student assessment policies, textbooks, course content, and offerings, whereas the curricula for higher-performing junior secondary schools are determined mainly by regional, local, or national educational authorities. The negative association between autonomy in curriculum and performance is statistically significant for mathematics but not for reading or science (table 7.7).

Table 7.7 Estimates of Mathematical, Reading, and Scientific Literacy Using School Characteristics, Junior Secondary

PISA variable	Mathematics		Reading		Science	
	Coefficient	Standard error	Coefficient	Standard error	Coefficient	Standard error
Organization, competition, and policy						
public	−67.73	15.552***	−61.05	13.018***	−28.98	12.954
compete	−4.00	12.631	−3.42	10.196	−8.56	10.338
academic	5.70	12.995	6.18	11.888	6.08	9.192
abg_math	−12.89	15.591				
mixed	−16.04	11.003	−14.68	9.546	−13.79	9.826
Teacher						
STRATIO	−1.12	0.827	−0.29	1.029	−1.12	0.907
PROPQUAL	−8.26	47.532	7.58	41.106	−1.76	42.584
TCMORALE	6.13	3.679	2.47	3.470	3.35	3.602
Shortage	7.46	9.688	20.50	9.482*	5.30	8.318
Resources						
SCMATEDU	0.65	4.576	4.98	4.139	−1.12	3.969
SCMATBUI	1.83	5.420	−2.79	5.236	2.56	4.910
COMPWEB	34.64	45.579	23.91	47.153	51.95	48.990
CLSIZE	0.15	0.387	0.19	0.366	0.26	0.455
CREACTIV	13.18	4.188**	10.88	3.810**	13.06	3.550***
Autonomy						
RESPRES	0.10	7.588	0.99	6.451	10.11	8.840
RESPCUR	−13.84	6.857*	−8.14	7.644	−11.80	6.582
Accountability						
Ppressure	9.73	9.897	9.54	8.457	7.33	8.215
scoretrack	−3.32	9.856	−9.86	8.855	−7.54	9.389
Climate						
STUDCLIM	4.30	2.976	4.29	2.176	3.68	2.798
TEACCLIM	−5.66	4.123	−4.96	3.120	−5.40	3.721
Leadership						
LEADCOM	−9.02	7.741	−3.69	6.088	−7.09	5.430
LEADINST	−0.72	7.643	−2.17	7.424	−2.81	6.990
LEADPD	−3.01	5.491	−5.06	5.236	−0.66	5.292
LEADTCH	5.99	8.443	5.31	7.173	2.10	7.164
N	2190		2190		2190	
R^2	0.349		0.368		0.343	

Source: Data from OECD 2012, PISA 2012 database (http://pisa2012.acer.edu.au/).
Note: See variable descriptions in table 7A.1. All models control for individual and family background characteristics, as well as grade-level fixed effects. PISA = Programme for International Student Assessment.
*$p < 0.05$, **$p < 0.01$, ***$p < 0.001$.

Senior Secondary General

Among measures of school resources, quality of school educational resources is significantly and positively related to reading scores in general senior secondary schools (table 7.8). Echoing the previous finding that model or experimental secondary schools have larger class sizes than ordinary ones, among general secondary school students, a one unit (student) increase in class size is associated with a 1.5 point higher score on mathematics and reading, after controlling for individual and family background characteristics. Among four dimensions of school leadership measures, levels of teacher participation in school leadership are positively and significantly associated with mathematical and reading literacy.

After controlling for individual and other school characteristics, students from mixed secondary schools perform significantly worse across all three domains than those from nonmixed general secondary schools. Furthermore, ability grouping between mathematics classes is associated with lower performance among secondary school students.

Senior Secondary Vocational

For vocational school students, reading scores do not seem to be significantly correlated with school-level characteristics after controlling for individual and family characteristics (table 7.9). Mathematics performance is, on the one hand, correlated with school accountability to parents: students attending schools that face pressure from parents score on average 41 points higher on mathematics. On the other hand, vocational schools with lower mathematics scores report significantly more student-related factors affecting school climate.

Science performance is significantly and positively related to several measures of school resources, including quality of physical infrastructure, class size, and availability of extracurricular creative activities at vocational senior secondary schools.

Individual and Family Background Characteristics

To demonstrate the correlation with individual and family background characteristics, school fixed effects models are used to estimate student performance (table 7.10).[2] We find a highly significant correlation between background characteristics and performance across all domains.

Girls perform worse on mathematics and science and better on reading compared with boys. Wealth is negatively correlated with performance. In comparison, more family educational resources and cultural possessions are associated with better performance. Similar results are found in other OECD countries, suggesting that on the one hand, family wealth can improve performance by providing more educational and cultural resources, but on the other hand, weakens students' incentives to learn and reduces the cost of leisure relative to education (Spiezia 2011). Parental education is also positively related to performance. Finally, students who have attended at least a year of preschool have a significant advantage across all domains over

Table 7.8 Estimates of Mathematical, Reading, and Scientific Literacy Using School Characteristics, Senior Secondary General Students

PISA variable	Mathematics		Reading		Science	
	Coefficient	Standard error	Coefficient	Standard error	Coefficient	Standard error
Organization, competition, and policy						
public	18.99	30.902	2.29	24.317	10.75	28.403
compete	11.52	19.660	22.04	14.438	10.08	14.761
academic	1.63	12.044	5.53	9.225	6.36	11.155
abg_math	−37.59	10.819***				
mixed	−31.88	13.880*	−34.02	8.429***	−23.30	8.910*
Teacher						
STRATIO	1.58	1.266	1.94	1.336	0.84	1.368
PROPQUAL	67.55	156.502	105.35	142.942	122.46	192.002
TCMORALE	4.62	6.063	2.31	4.616	4.76	5.024
Shortage	1.46	9.339	5.69	6.187	13.22	9.939
Resources						
SCMATEDU	4.80	6.134	10.34	4.586*	3.99	5.450
SCMATBUI	2.23	5.720	−4.16	4.417	2.73	4.480
COMPWEB	35.98	54.906	39.21	55.913	42.62	58.661
CLSIZE	1.51	0.752*	1.56	0.581**	0.44	0.819
CREACTIV	13.70	7.936	5.60	5.280	7.74	6.038
Autonomy						
RESPRES	15.38	12.577	5.69	10.328	7.16	10.809
RESPCUR	−7.24	11.760	−4.74	8.418	−5.66	8.502
Accountability						
Ppressure	12.15	10.180	13.02	7.868	2.17	8.867
scoretrack	10.74	9.858	−0.56	7.816	5.78	8.086
Climate						
STUDCLIM	2.33	4.479	−1.17	3.456	0.22	3.307
TEACCLIM	−2.58	5.623	0.62	4.523	−0.71	4.908
Leadership						
LEADCOM	−5.69	9.102	−0.52	7.573	−6.79	7.589
LEADINST	4.03	7.428	3.67	6.067	4.27	6.196
LEADPD	−11.82	9.151	−7.12	7.612	−5.92	7.151
LEADTCH	21.34	8.198*	15.08	6.772*	6.43	7.871
N	1632		1632		1632	
R^2	0.227		0.215		0.176	

Source: Data from OECD 2012, PISA 2012 database (http://pisa2012.acer.edu.au/).
Note: See variable descriptions in table 7A.1. All models control for individual and family background characteristics, as well as grade-level fixed effects. PISA = Programme for International Student Assessment.
*$p < 0.05$, **$p < 0.01$, ***$p < 0.001$.

Table 7.9 Estimates of Mathematical, Reading, and Scientific Literacy Using School Characteristics, Senior Secondary Vocational

PISA variable	Mathematics		Reading		Science	
	Coefficient	Standard error	Coefficient	Standard error	Coefficient	Standard error
Individual and family characteristics						
female	−17.10	5.186**	20.60	4.875**	−13.83	4.995**
WEALTH	−12.17	4.016**	−6.69	3.400	−9.53	3.508**
HEDRES	6.06	3.220	5.57	2.222*	5.29	2.329*
CULTPOS	5.13	3.061	3.69	2.394	7.73	2.472**
PARED	1.95	0.831*	1.98	0.726**	1.84	0.636**
preschool	28.33	7.672***	21.86	5.478***	16.30	5.975**
Organization, competition, and policy						
public	−67.85	56.197	12.79	40.016	−0.32	36.582
compete	−37.81	33.852	−9.39	26.961	30.28	28.534
academic	−0.51	18.558	5.29	12.087	4.17	15.045
abg_math	−7.20	29.901				
Teacher						
STRATIO	1.13	0.800	0.98	0.580	0.82	0.704
PROPQUAL	159.09	116.643	14.65	106.227	59.53	89.438
TCMORALE	0.21	4.696	5.01	4.668	4.54	4.411
Shortage	19.37	13.152	11.71	11.603	20.03	11.047
Resources						
SCMATEDU	1.95	4.251	3.53	4.123	−0.44	4.118
SCMATBUI	1.68	4.743	−1.61	3.710	8.81	4.263*
COMPWEB	13.07	48.016	7.32	27.565	4.75	26.475
CLSIZE	−0.05	1.362	0.79	0.696	1.87	0.930*
CREACTIV	6.39	10.015	4.83	8.278	17.34	6.748*
Autonomy						
RESPRES	16.53	10.885	3.17	7.573	−4.68	7.341
RESPCUR	2.53	4.756	−3.62	4.366	−6.86	4.783
Accountability						
Ppressure	41.82	18.154*	4.69	15.448	7.85	11.951
scoretrack	−5.05	9.330	7.12	7.186	0.68	6.799
Climate						
STUDCLIM	−14.71	7.046*	−2.90	6.834	−0.63	7.340
TEACCLIM	7.12	5.260	−0.79	4.414	−3.89	4.822
Leadership						
LEADCOM	−14.10	9.693	2.51	7.646	−5.14	8.032
LEADINST	13.78	18.216	14.17	13.496	5.80	12.774
LEADPD	8.43	13.505	−4.49	9.420	13.76	8.678
LEADTCH	5.95	9.848	1.89	6.245	−10.48	7.180
N	1070		1070		1070	
R^2	0.156		0.166		0.155	

Source: Data from OECD 2012, PISA 2012 database (http://pisa2012.acer.edu.au/).
Note: See variable descriptions in table 7A.1. All models control for individual and family background characteristics, as well as grade-level fixed effects. PISA = Programme for International Student Assessment.
*$p < 0.05$, **$p < 0.01$, ***$p < 0.001$.

Table 7.10 Estimates of Mathematical, Reading, and Scientific Literacy Using Individual and Household Background Characteristics, Controlling for School Fixed Effects

PISA variable	Mathematics		Reading		Science	
	Coefficient	Standard error	Coefficient	Standard error	Coefficient	Standard error
female	−17.89	2.268***	13.27	1.650***	−15.53	2.101***
WEALTH	−6.96	1.664***	−5.49	1.633**	−5.87	1.417***
HEDRES	4.62	1.560**	4.19	1.238**	4.95	1.301***
CULTPOS	6.11	1.630***	4.94	1.222***	8.40	1.250***
PARED	1.40	0.426**	1.21	0.367**	1.44	0.374***
preschool	31.12	3.879***	21.30	3.265***	16.36	3.151***
N	4892		4892		4892	
R^2	0.54		0.54		0.54	

Source: Data from OECD 2012, PISA 2012 database (http://pisa2012.acer.edu.au/).
Note: See variable descriptions in table 7A.1. All models control for fixed effects and grade-level fixed effects.
PISA = Programme for International Student Assessment.
*$p < 0.05$, **$p < 0.01$, ***$p < 0.001$.

those who have not: the differences range from 16 points in science to as many as 31 points in mathematics, even after controlling for gender and other family background characteristics.

Problem-Solving Skills

Shanghai ranks sixth on overall problem-solving skills on PISA 2012. As displayed in figure 7.4, students in Singapore, Korea, and Japan, followed by students in Hong Kong SAR, China, and Macao SAR, China, score higher in problem solving than students in all other participating countries and economies. Disaggregation of data reveals that students in Hong Kong SAR, China; Japan; Korea; Macao SAR, China; Shanghai; Singapore; and Taiwan, China, perform strongest on problems that require understanding, formulating, or representing new knowledge, compared with other types of problems. At the same time, students in Brazil, Ireland, Korea, and the United States perform strongest on interactive problems that require students to uncover some of the information needed to solve the problem, compared with static problems for which all information is disclosed at the outset (OECD 2014).

Estimating Problem-Solving Skills Using School Characteristics

The same set of school-level characteristics is used to estimate problem-solving scores (Model 1), controlling for student and family background (table 7.11).

The problem-solving assessment of PISA 2012 was designed to focus as much as possible on cognitive processes and generic skills rather than domain-specific knowledge (OECD 2014). However, because the same cognitive processes can also be used in mathematics, science, and reading, problem-solving scores are positively correlated with the other three domains. For students in Shanghai, as much as 71 percent of the problem-solving score reflects skills that are also

Figure 7.4 Problem Solving, Mean Score, PISA 2012

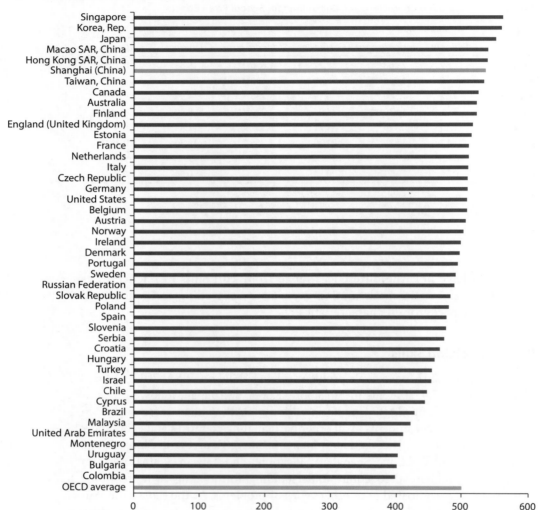

Sources: Data from OECD 2012, PISA 2012 database (http://pisa2012.acer.edu.au/); OECD 2014.
Note: OECD = Organisation for Economic Co-operation and Development; PISA = Programme for International Student Assessment.

measured in at least one of the three regular assessment domains; 64.8 percent of the variance in problem-solving scores is associated with more than one regular domain, and 5.8 percent of the variance is uniquely associated with mathematics (OECD 2014). Because problem-solving skills are highly correlated with performance in the mathematics, reading, and science domains, which are related to school-level characteristics, to account for omitted variable bias, mathematics, reading, and science scores are controlled for in the full models (Model 2) used to estimate problem-solving scores.

For junior secondary students, after controlling for math, reading, and science scores, problem-solving skills are significantly and positively related to quality of

Table 7.11 **Estimates of Problem-Solving Skills Using School Characteristics**

PISA variable	Junior secondary				Senior secondary general				Senior secondary vocational			
	Model 1		Model 2		Model 1		Model 2		Model 1		Model 2	
	Coefficient	Standard error	Coefficient	Standard error	Coefficient	Standard error	Coefficient	Standard error	Coefficient	Standard error	Coefficient	Standard error
Individual and family background												
female	−34.73	3.101***	−34.83	3.229***	−36.48	3.052***	−28.86	3.371***	−29.34	5.236***	−30.51	4.052***
WEALTH	3.59	2.585	7.64	1.554***	2.24	2.774	6.02	2.028**	−2.56	3.719	5.38	1.961**
HEDRES	9.38	2.331***	2.08	1.434	4.41	2.149*	2.49	1.581	8.43	2.599**	3.20	1.394*
CULTPOS	1.63	2.287	−6.48	1.481***	−6.33	2.757*	−6.66	1.732***	−3.30	2.659	−6.59	1.493***
PARED	2.05	0.784*	0.29	0.403	3.06	0.887***	0.51	0.711	2.00	0.705**	0.29	0.516
preschool	30.56	5.182***	0.64	3.268	27.59	6.839***	11.99	4.790*	31.42	6.494***	9.20	4.385*
Organization, competition, and policy												
public	−34.43	19.102	23.39	13.083	11.86	29.761	1.45	22.571	−103.47	34.691**	−53.80	41.634
compete	−2.38	10.367	1.21	11.182	31.84	14.114*	17.22	10.892	−32.46	18.600	−0.44	27.297
academic	−2.56	11.124	−8.82	10.201	3.05	14.629	−3.18	11.955	18.89	13.366	13.14	19.956
mixed	−4.40	12.634	7.92	12.276	−23.69	13.202	3.30	10.237				
Teacher												
STRATIO	0.04	0.961	1.00	0.851	3.13	1.495*	1.43	1.733	−1.35	0.858	−2.24	1.047*
PROPQUAL	−36.62	42.847	−24.82	37.025	167.40	152.501	130.03	103.232	−34.89	92.405	−173.50	97.933
TCMORALE	6.94	5.178	3.46	4.176	9.01	6.041	5.83	4.681	−3.53	6.864	−5.15	5.862
TCSHORT	0.00	0.002	0.00	0.002	0.23	4.057	1.85	4.459	−5.00	9.602	−6.79	8.049
Resources												
SCMATEDU	8.04	4.305	7.84	3.294*	2.90	5.788	−1.36	5.782	−10.45	9.136	−11.51	8.133
SCMATBUI	−5.67	5.176	−5.90	3.528	9.07	7.291	8.83	6.102	−8.42	5.451	−8.02	5.582

table continues next page

Table 7.11 Estimates of Problem-Solving Skills Using School Characteristics (continued)

| | Junior secondary | | | | Senior secondary general | | | | Senior secondary vocational | | | |
| | Model 1 | | Model 2 | | Model 1 | | Model 2 | | Model 1 | | Model 2 | |
PISA variable	Coefficient	Standard error	Coefficient	Standard error	Coefficient	Standard error	Coefficient	Standard error	Coefficient	Standard error	Coefficient	Standard error
COMPWEB	54.06	51.119	31.38	52.898	19.86	41.137	−19.53	63.312	−1.81	35.836	−20.23	30.225
CLSIZE	0.49	0.501	0.40	0.513	0.33	1.072	−0.88	0.876	−1.26	0.955	−1.38	0.656*
CREACTIV	8.01	4.433	−1.38	3.745	7.10	9.612	0.50	6.127	13.22	9.819	13.54	13.641
Autonomy												
RESPRES	9.15	8.490	11.03	6.268	11.34	11.146	3.67	7.915	1.58	7.352	−9.42	6.621
RESPCUR	−1.52	8.247	6.72	4.264	−10.34	10.693	−3.94	6.416	27.07	8.400**	26.90	8.146**
Accountability												
Ppressure	3.26	10.428	−5.56	7.921	17.60	10.149	4.65	11.810	35.78	17.350*	5.34	13.622
scoretrack	−4.17	10.580	−1.12	10.931	−2.28	7.721	−7.28	7.668	−23.57	10.338*	−26.30	10.103*
Climate												
STUDCLIM	4.99	4.971	1.11	4.155	3.74	4.813	2.20	3.102	−7.80	6.678	−0.08	7.195
TEACCLIM	−12.30	6.463	−6.70	5.766	−6.59	5.936	−4.38	3.771	14.71	7.613	11.22	8.100
Leadership												
LEADCOM	1.38	7.918	6.27	8.485	−0.02	10.276	4.29	7.516	13.37	11.561	17.33	12.987
LEADINST	12.01	6.480	13.63	6.198*	−10.02	7.642	−12.85	7.655	−34.37	16.177	−54.36	12.138***
LEADPD	−4.89	6.775	−1.63	6.300	−5.10	7.643	3.74	5.396	21.60	10.871	26.43	10.689*
LEADTCH	−2.67	6.366	−7.08	6.265	14.28	10.939	−0.23	9.165	1.74	10.118	−0.97	7.687
Main domain performance												
Mathematics			0.52	0.047***			0.48	0.047***			0.49	0.040***
Reading			0.40	0.067***			0.36	0.067***			0.41	0.076***
Science			−0.09	0.055			−0.01	0.058			−0.07	0.064
N	2224		2224		1632		1632		1070		1070	

Source: Data from OECD 2012, PISA 2012 database (http://pisa2012.acer.edu.au/).

Note: See variable descriptions in table 7A.1. All models contain grade-level fixed effects. PISA = Programme for International Student Assessment.

$*p < 0.05$, $**p < 0.01$, $***p < 0.001$.

school educational resources, as well as to principals' instructional leadership, measured by how often principals promote teaching practices based on recent educational research, praise teachers, and draw teachers' attention to the importance of pupils' development.

For general senior secondary students, although student-to-teacher ratios and competition from other schools seem to be related to higher problem-solving scores in Model 1, the relationship seems to be accounted for in part by performances on mathematics, reading, and science, given that the coefficients become small and no longer statistically significant once performance on the three regular domains is controlled for in Model 2.

The most interesting results are found among vocational senior secondary students. After controlling for student and family background, public school students score as much as 103 points lower on problem-solving skills than do private school students. The gap seems to be accounted for in part by performance in mathematics, reading, and science, seeing as the size of the coefficient is halved and no longer statistically significant once differences in the three main domains are accounted for. Holding mathematics, reading, and science performance constant, student-to-teacher ratio and class size are negatively correlated with problem-solving scores.

Vocational schools whose curriculum and assessment policies are determined by school councils, principals, or teachers, as opposed to national, regional, or local educational authorities, score higher on problem-solving skills, even after controlling for mathematical, reading, and scientific literacy.

Between the two accountability measures, vocational schools faced with parental pressure score higher on problem solving, but the difference goes away once mathematical, reading, and scientific literacy are accounted for. In comparison, vocational schools whose academic performance is tracked by an education authority score lower on problem solving, and the difference remains even after accounting for mathematical, reading, and scientific literacy.

Among various dimensions of school leadership, vocational schools with better problem-solving performance see principals more often promoting institutional improvements and professional development, but less often demonstrating instructional leadership (by promoting teaching practices, praising teachers, and drawing teachers' attention to the importance of pupils' development).

Among student and family background characteristics, girls in every type of program score lower than boys on problem solving, and the size of the difference does not seem to change much after differences in mathematical, reading, and scientific literacy are accounted for. This finding suggests that girls' disadvantages in problem-solving skills might be independent of their lower mathematics and science performance observed before.

Family wealth only has a significant and positive effect on problem solving after adjusting for performance in the three main domains. Similarly, family cultural possessions have a negative and significant correlation with problem-solving scores after we control for mathematics, reading, and science scores. The positive relationship between home educational resources and problem-solving skills is no longer statistically significant once mathematical, reading, and scientific literacy are accounted for, except for vocational school students. Students who have attended at least a year of preschool score higher on problem solving in all three types of programs, but the advantage goes away once differences in mathematical, reading, and scientific literacy are accounted for.

Problem Solving by Nature and Process: Comparing Problem-Solving Skills by Nature, Process, and Program

This section takes an in-depth look at problem-solving skills by nature of the problem situation and the different problem-solving processes, as measured by PISA 2012 (box 7.2). First the solution rates[3] on each specific type of problem are compared. Then logistic regression models are used to predict the solution rates with the same set of school characteristics.

Senior secondary general school students have the highest solution rates on both static and interactive problems (figure 7.5). Vocational students have

---

Box 7.2 Definitions and Implications of the Nature and Processes of Problem Solving

PISA 2012 defines problem-solving competence as an individual's capacity to engage in cognitive processing to understand and resolve problem situations where a method of solution is not immediately obvious. It includes the willingness to engage with such situations in order to achieve one's potential as a constructive and reflective citizen.

Nature of the problem situation

- *Static problems:* Information disclosed to the student at the outset is sufficient to solve the problem. These are the typical textbook problems encountered in schools.
- *Interactive problems:* Interaction with the problem situation is a necessary part of the solving activity. These are the types of problems encountered in most contexts outside of schools. To excel in interactive tasks, it is not sufficient to possess the problem-solving skills required by static, analytical problems; students must also be open to novelty, tolerate doubt and uncertainty, and dare to use intuition ("hunches and feelings") to initiate a solution.

Problem-solving processes

Knowledge-acquisition tasks require students to generate and manipulate the information in a mental representation. The movement is from concrete to abstract, from information to knowledge. Students who are strong on these tasks are good at generating new knowledge; they can be characterized as quick learners, who are highly inquisitive (questioning their own knowledge, challenging assumptions), generating and experimenting with alternatives, and good at abstract information processing.

box continues next page

Box 7.2 Definitions and Implications of the Nature and Processes of Problem Solving *(continued)*

- ***Exploring and understanding*** involves exploring the problem situation by observing it, interacting with it, searching for information, and finding limitations or obstacles; and demonstrating understanding of the information given and the information discovered while interacting with the problem situation.

- ***Representing and formulating*** involves using tables, graphs, symbols, or words to represent aspects of the problem situation; and formulating hypotheses about the relevant factors in a problem and the relationships between them, to build a coherent mental representation of the problem situation.

Knowledge-utilization tasks require students to solve a concrete problem. The movement is from abstract to concrete, from knowledge to action. Students who are good at tasks whose main cognitive demand is "planning and executing" are good at using the knowledge they have; they can be characterized as goal-driven and persistent.

- ***Planning and executing*** involves devising a plan or strategy to solve the problem, and executing it. It may involve clarifying the overall goal, and setting subgoals.

- ***Monitoring and reflecting*** involves monitoring progress, reacting to feedback, and reflecting on the solution, the information provided with the problem, or the strategy adopted. It combines both knowledge-acquisition and knowledge-utilization aspects.

Source: Adapted from OECD 2014.

Figure 7.5 Solution Rates on PISA Items Measuring Different Natures and Processes of Problem Solving, by Program

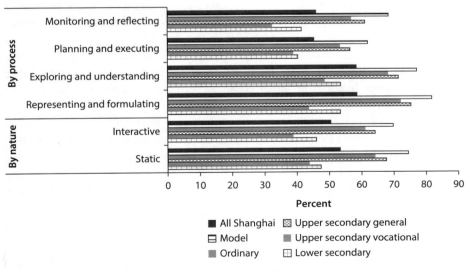

Source: Data from OECD 2012, PISA 2012 database (http://pisa2012.acer.edu.au/).
Note: PISA = Programme for International Student Assessment.

significantly lower solution rates on interactive problems, even compared with junior secondary students. Among general senior secondary students, model or experimental school students have significantly higher solution rates than ordinary school students on both types of problems.

Senior secondary general students also have higher solution rates on all four types of problems measuring different problem-solving processes, while vocational students have the lowest solution rates. The gap is particularly pronounced (a 32 percentage point difference) on items involving "representing and formulating." Model secondary school students have higher solution rates on all four kinds of problem-solving processes than do ordinary secondary school students, and the advantage is most pronounced on "monitoring and reflecting" questions (12 percentage point difference).

Estimating Odds Ratio for Success, by Nature and Process
Nature of Problems: Static versus Interactive
PISA tested students on problem-solving tasks of two distinctive natures: the static problems are typical "textbook" problems that can be solved by using information disclosed at the outset, whereas interactive problems often require students to uncover the information necessary for solving the problem.

Despite the distinctive natures of the problem-solving tasks, the regression models seem to demonstrate similar associations with school-level characteristics (table 7.12). For example, for both static and interactive problems, public school students have 34 percent lower odds of receiving full credit. Mixed secondary school students also have a disadvantage on both static and interactive problem solving.

Teacher qualities do not seem to have a significant relationship with either static or interactive problem solving, except that higher teacher morale is associated with slightly higher odds of students succeeding in solving static problems.

Among school resource measures, the more creative extracurricular activities available at a school, the more likely students are to succeed in solving either type of problem. In addition, larger class size is related to slightly higher odds of succeeding on static problem solving.

Schools with better performance on interactive problems also report more student-related factors that disrupt school climate, consistent with the descriptive findings that principals of better-performing schools might be more aware of students' disruptive behaviors. Teacher-related factors that affect school climate are associated with a lower probability of students successfully solving either type of problem.

Among background characteristics, girls are significantly less likely to succeed in problem solving than boys, regardless of the nature of the problems. Home educational resources are associated with higher odds of solving interactive problems, whereas cultural possessions are associated with higher odds of solving static problems. Students who have attended preschool for at least a year are more likely to solve interactive problems than those who have not.

Table 7.12 Estimates of Odds Ratios for Success, by Nature of Problem

PISA variable	Static		Interactive	
	Coefficient	Standard error	Coefficient	Standard error
Individual and family background				
female	0.71	0.046***	0.73	0.048***
WEALTH	1.07	0.064	1.06	0.049
HEDRES	1.01	0.047	1.09	0.043*
CULTPOS	1.11	0.046*	0.97	0.037
PARED	1.00	0.015	1.02	0.012
preschool	1.15	0.136	1.37	0.160*
Organization, competition, and policy				
public	0.66	0.126*	0.66	0.115
compete	0.99	0.093	0.98	0.110
academic	1.13	0.111	1.02	0.085
mixed	0.78	0.066**	0.81	0.073*
Teacher				
STRATIO	1.00	0.008	1.00	0.007
PROPQUAL	0.90	0.503	1.20	0.624
TCMORALE	1.11	0.053*	1.01	0.035
TCSHORT	1.00	0.000	1.00	0.000
Resources				
SCMATEDU	1.01	0.056	0.99	0.034
SCMATBUI	0.96	0.049	1.06	0.042
COMPWEB	1.14	0.333	1.35	0.383
CLSIZE	1.01	0.004*	1.00	0.004
CREACTIV	1.17	0.060**	1.11	0.049*
Autonomy				
RESPRES	1.01	0.069	1.08	0.058
RESPCUR	0.96	0.049	1.00	0.046
Accountability				
Ppressure	1.06	0.111	1.10	0.085
scoretrack	0.99	0.075	0.95	0.073
Climate				
STUDCLIM	1.06	0.038	1.08	0.034*
TEACCLIM	0.91	0.036*	0.89	0.033**
Leadership				
LEADCOM	0.90	0.060	1.05	0.058
LEADINST	0.98	0.066	1.03	0.057
LEADPD	0.94	0.064	0.94	0.050
LEADTCH	1.04	0.069	1.02	0.054
Program				
General high	1.93	0.230***	1.81	0.194
Vocational high	0.82	0.119	0.74	0.089*
N	1,145		1,145	

Source: Data from OECD 2012, PISA 2012 database (http://pisa2012.acer.edu.au/).
Note: See variable descriptions in table 7A.1. PISA = Programme for International Student Assessment.
*$p < 0.05$, **$p < 0.01$, ***$p < 0.001$.

After accounting for student and school characteristics, attending a general secondary school almost doubles the odds of solving static problems over junior secondary schools, and the difference is statistically significant. In comparison, vocational school students are much less likely, on average, than junior secondary school students to solve interactive problems, and the difference is statistically significant.

Problem-Solving Process

The various items on the PISA problem-solving test also distinguish between knowledge-acquisition and knowledge-utilization tasks, each of which incorporate two problem-solving processes. Knowledge-acquisition tasks, corresponding to "exploring and understanding" and "representing and formulating" processes, require students to generate new, abstract knowledge by processing and manipulating information. Knowledge-utilization tasks, in contrast, correspond to "planning and executing" and require students to use abstract knowledge to solve concrete problems. In addition, items that involve "monitoring and reflecting" tasks test students on both knowledge acquisition and knowledge utilization.

Among knowledge-acquisition tasks, the odds ratio for items involving "representing and formulating" does not seem to vary by school characteristics after controlling for background characteristics and the fixed effects of different programs (table 7.13). For items requiring "exploring and understanding" processes, several school-level characteristics are associated with higher success rates: students from schools that use academic criteria for admission (achievement or recommendations from feeder schools) are more

Table 7.13 Estimates of Odds Ratio for Success, by Problem-Solving Process

PISA variable	Representing and formulating		Exploring and understanding		Planning and executing		Monitoring and reflecting	
	Coefficient	Standard error	Coefficient	Standard error	Coefficient	Standard error	Coefficient	Standard error
Individual and family background								
female	0.54	0.047***	0.84	0.069*	0.75	0.065**	0.83	0.075*
WEALTH	1.10	0.077	1.09	0.063	1.04	0.061	1.02	0.069
HEDRES	1.09	0.056	1.04	0.051	1.07	0.054	0.99	0.060
CULTPOS	1.05	0.058	1.02	0.056	0.97	0.038	1.12	0.066
PARED	1.04	0.019*	0.99	0.015	1.01	0.014	1.02	0.018
preschool	1.17	0.195	1.27	0.183	1.35	0.173*	1.53	0.218**
Organization, competition, and policy								
public	0.76	0.166	0.61	0.163	0.72	0.093*	0.59	0.119*
compete	0.92	0.162	0.96	0.113	1.16	0.094	0.80	0.096
academic	0.98	0.118	1.27	0.135*	0.94	0.072	1.06	0.116
mixed	0.79	0.106	0.87	0.084	0.81	0.070*	0.72	0.082**

table continues next page

Table 7.13 Estimates of Odds Ratio for Success, by Problem-Solving Process (continued)

PISA variable	Representing and formulating		Exploring and understanding		Planning and executing		Monitoring and reflecting	
	Coefficient	Standard error	Coefficient	Standard error	Coefficient	Standard error	Coefficient	Standard error
Teacher								
STRATIO	1.01	0.012	0.99	0.009	1.00	0.008	1.00	0.009
PROPQUAL	3.11	2.223	0.79	0.490	0.71	0.285	0.76	0.486
TCMORALE	1.04	0.057	1.07	0.055	1.05	0.038	0.99	0.054
TCSHORT	1.00	0.000	1.00	0.000	1.00	0.000*	1.00	0.000**
Resources								
SCMATEDU	0.98	0.052	1.05	0.049	0.98	0.039	0.93	0.046
SCMATBUI	1.01	0.059	0.97	0.056	1.08	0.045	1.06	0.056
COMPWEB	1.39	0.563	1.49	0.432	1.10	0.254	1.58	0.495
CLSIZE	1.00	0.007	1.01	0.005	1.00	0.003	1.00	0.004
CREACTIV	1.11	0.072	1.17	0.067*	1.10	0.047*	1.18	0.065**
Autonomy								
RESPRES	1.21	0.143	1.02	0.073	1.00	0.041	1.08	0.084
RESPCUR	0.92	0.070	1.04	0.056	0.99	0.043	0.97	0.068
Accountability								
Ppressure	1.15	0.131	1.14	0.124	0.93	0.068	1.30	0.145*
scoretrack	0.99	0.108	0.89	0.090	1.00	0.065	0.99	0.091
Climate								
STUDCLIM	1.09	0.056	1.10	0.045*	1.07	0.029*	1.02	0.046
TEACCLIM	0.90	0.053	0.88	0.044*	0.90	0.029**	0.97	0.052
Leadership								
LEADCOM	1.01	0.098	0.99	0.064	0.99	0.047	1.03	0.100
LEADINST	1.08	0.094	0.94	0.075	0.97	0.055	1.19	0.100*
LEADPD	0.89	0.078	1.01	0.064	0.99	0.050	0.86	0.063*
LEADTCH	1.02	0.084	0.99	0.067	1.03	0.042	1.01	0.091
Program								
General high	2.28	0.375***	1.67	0.219***	1.78	0.183***	1.96	0.251***
Vocational high	0.72	0.149	0.77	0.103	0.94	0.119	0.64	0.104**
N	1145		1145		1145		1145	

Source: Data from OECD 2012, PISA 2012 database (http://pisa2012.acer.edu.au/).
Note: See variable descriptions in table 7A.1. PISA = Programme for International Student Assessment.
*$p < 0.05$, **$p < 0.01$, ***$p < 0.001$.

likely to succeed; creative extracurricular activities available in school are also associated with higher success ratios.

Similar to findings on interactive problem solving, schools that report more student-related factors affecting school climate actually have better performance on both "exploring and understanding" and "planning and executing" tasks, whereas reported teacher-related factors are associated with lower success rates on the same types of problem. Creative extracurricular activities and school climate measures exhibit similar relationships with success ratios on "planning and executing" questions, which correspond to knowledge-utilization tasks. In addition, public school students show a disadvantage in accomplishing knowledge-utilization tasks involving "planning and executing" compared with private school students.

For "monitoring and reflecting" processes that involve both knowledge-acquisition and -utilization tasks, public school students have 41 percent lower odds of gaining full credit than private school students. Pressure from parents and creative activities available at school are both positively related to the odds of solving "monitoring and reflecting" questions. Among measures of school leadership, principal's instructional leadership shows a positive relationship with the odds of solving the "monitoring and reflecting" questions. However, promoting instructional improvements and professional development, as measured by how often a principal takes the initiative to discuss, pay attention to, and help teachers solve classroom problems, actually shows a negative relationship with students' odds of solving "monitoring and reflecting" problems.

Among individual characteristics, girls are less likely than boys to succeed across all four problem-solving processes, and the gap is particularly large for "representing and formulating" questions that correspond to knowledge-acquisition tasks. Students who have attended at least a year of preschool are significantly more likely to solve "planning and execution" problems and "monitoring and reflecting" problems than those who have not. Family background characteristics do not seem to have a significant relationship with the success ratio on any specific problem-solving process, except that parental education level is associated with a higher probability of solving "representing and formulating" questions.

Summary

Examining student learning outcomes using PISA scores and their correlation with school- and individual-level characteristics sheds further light on how Shanghai's educational policies and their implementation across schools can have an impact on student learning outcomes.

Mathematical, Reading, and Scientific Literacy

The performance of students in Shanghai shows great variation across academic programs. Particularly, the mean scores of vocational students are not only lower than those of general senior secondary students but also those of junior secondary students on all three domains (mathematics, reading, science). Students attending model or experimental secondary schools perform the best in all three domains. It must be emphasized that the variation across programs is partly accounted for by the admissions process that places students on the general versus vocational educational track by performance on the *zhong kao*.

Individual and family background characteristics differ significantly across academic programs. Compared with vocational students, general senior secondary students come from wealthier families with more home educational resources, cultural possessions, and higher levels of parental education. They are also more likely to have attended at least a year of preschool. General senior secondary students attending model or experimental secondary schools enjoy higher levels of family wealth, home educational resources, and parental education levels than do those attending ordinary secondary schools.

At the school level, the main differences between general secondary schools and vocational secondary schools lie in their teaching resources: general secondary schools are characterized by much lower student-to-teacher ratios and higher proportions of teachers with tertiary qualifications. Moreover, whereas the vast majority of general secondary schools use academic achievement as admission criteria, only 60 percent of vocational schools do so. Model or experimental secondary schools and ordinary secondary schools do not differ significantly on school-level characteristics except for the larger class sizes and student-to-teacher ratios of the former.

How are school-level characteristics associated with variation in students' mathematical, reading, and scientific literacy? The correlation between school characteristics and student performance within each program (junior secondary, senior secondary general, senior secondary vocational) was investigated. Among junior secondary students, schools with more creative extracurricular activities available were found to perform better across all three domains. Consistent with what was found in 2009, private school students (accounting for 10 percent of the total junior secondary student population) perform significantly better than public school students on mathematics and reading. Moreover, junior secondary schools with more autonomy in determining curriculum and assessment actually perform worse in mathematics.

Among senior secondary students, teacher participation in school leadership is significantly related to higher mathematics and reading scores. The quality of school educational resources is also positively related to reading performance. The 2009 PISA data show a higher level of teacher participation in school governance and better educational resources among better-performing schools. In addition, ability grouping in mathematics is related to lower mathematics scores among senior secondary students. Finally, students of mixed schools perform significantly lower than students of nonmixed schools in all three domains.

Among vocational students, schools with better mathematics performance tend to have lower student-related factors affecting school climate, consistent with what was found in 2009. Schools facing pressure from parents have higher mean mathematics scores than those who do not. The scientific literacy of vocational school students is positively and significantly related to schools' quality of physical infrastructure, class size, and availability of creative extracurricular activities.

In addition, individual and family background characteristics demonstrate a consistent relationship with student performance across academic programs. Girls perform significantly worse on mathematics and science, and better on reading, than boys, consistent with findings from other countries and economies participating in PISA. Home educational resources, cultural possessions, and parental education levels exhibit a positive relationship with student literacy. In contrast, family wealth is negatively related to performance. Finally, students who have attended at least a year of preschool exhibit a significant academic advantage on all three domains.

Problem Solving

Similar to mathematics, reading, and science, test results on problem-solving skills among general senior secondary students compared with junior secondary students and vocational students were analyzed. Problem-solving skills in the models were measured by overall scores, as well as solution rates specific to the nature of problem solving (static vs. interactive) and process (representing and formulating, exploring and understanding, planning and executing, monitoring and reflecting). Model or experimental secondary school students demonstrate higher overall problem-solving scores and specific problem-solving skills than do ordinary secondary school students.

To begin, how school characteristics are related to overall problem-solving scores was investigated. Similar to the other domains, separate regression models were estimated for each academic program. Performance on mathematics, science, and reading was included in the model to see if the predictors have an independent effect on problem solving or if the association is mediated by performance on the three core domains.

For junior secondary students, problem-solving skills are significantly and positively related to quality of school educational resources and principals' instructional leadership, after accounting for mathematics, reading, and science performance.

For general senior secondary students, schools with higher student-to-teacher ratios and facing competition from other schools tend to have students who perform better on problem solving, although the relationship seems to be accounted for by differences in performance on mathematics, reading, and science.

Among vocational students, problem-solving skills are related to a number of school characteristics. Holding mathematics, science, and reading performance constant, vocational schools with smaller student-to-teacher ratios and class sizes have better problem-solving scores. Vocational schools with more autonomy over curriculum and assessment policies and whose academic performance is not tracked by an education authority perform better on problem solving, and the difference remains even after accounting for mathematical, reading, and scientific literacy. Among various dimensions of school leadership, schools with better problem-solving performance have principals who more often promote institutional improvements and professional development, but who less often demonstrate instructional leadership. There is a significant advantage in problem-solving skills among private vocational school students over public ones, but the gap seems to be accounted for by performance in mathematics, reading, and science. Similarly, vocational schools that encounter parental pressure score higher on problem solving, but the difference goes away once mathematical, reading, and scientific literacy are accounted for.

School characteristics are also used to predict success rates on specific types of problems. First, problem solving by nature of the task was examined. The analysis found that similar school characteristics are related to solution rates on both static and interactive problems. For example, public school students have significantly lower solution rates on both types of problems than private school students; more creative extracurricular activities available at school, and fewer teacher-related factors that affect school climate are related to higher solution rates on both types of problems. Several school characteristics seem to be significantly related to solution rates on problem solving of a specific nature. For example, larger class sizes are associated with slightly greater odds of students solving static problems, but the effect on interactive problem solving is not statistically significant.

We also examined the solution rates on problem-solving questions by the different types of problem-solving processes involved and found that the availability of creative extracurricular activities is positively related to success ratios on "exploring and understanding," "planning and executing," and "monitoring and reflecting" questions. Public school students show a disadvantage in both "planning and executing" and "monitoring and reflecting" processes compared with private school students. Among measures of school leadership, although the principal's instructional leadership shows a positive relationship with the success ratio on "monitoring and reflecting" questions, the promotion of instructional improvements and professional development actually shows a negative relationship with students' success ratios on this type of problem.

It is interesting that the analysis found that schools reporting more student-related factors that affect school climate in fact have students with higher problem-solving skills, particularly on interactive problem solving and certain problem-solving tasks such as "exploring and understanding" and "planning and executing." This finding should be interpreted with caution given that the measure of student-related factors is reported by school principals. The finding could suggest that principals from better-performing schools are simply more aware of students' disruptive behaviors. Or the finding could suggest that disruptive student behaviors might not indicate worse performance on certain dimensions of cognitive skills.

Among individual characteristics, girls have lower problem-solving skills than boys, regardless of specific nature or process, and the disadvantage seems to be independent of their disadvantage in mathematics and science.

After variances in mathematics, reading, and scientific literacy are accounted for, family wealth is significantly correlated with higher problem-solving scores, while family cultural possessions are negatively related to problem-solving scores. The positive relationship between home educational resources and problem-solving skills seems to be partially accounted for by variations in mathematical, reading, and scientific literacy.

Several family background characteristics are also associated with student skills in solving problems of a specific nature. For example, family cultural possessions are associated with higher odds of solving static problems, while home educational resources are associated with higher odds of solving interactive problems. Parental education level is associated with a higher probability of solving problems involving "representing and formulating" processes.

Students who have attended at least a year of preschool have better problem-solving scores, but the advantage seems to be accounted for by variations in mathematical, reading, and scientific literacy. Preschool attendance is also related to higher odds of solving interactive problems, and problems involving "planning and execution" and "monitoring and reflecting" processes.

Annex 7A

Table 7A.1 Description of PISA Variables

Variable	Description
abg_math	1 = Ability grouping for some or all mathematics classes; 0 = no ability grouping for any mathematics classes
academic	1 = always consider academic performance or recommendation from feeder school; 0 = never or sometimes consider
CLSIZE	Class size
compete	1 = face competition from at least one other school; 0 = no others
COMPWEB	Ratio of computers connected to web and number of computers
CREACTIV	Index of creative extracurricular activities at school
	Total number of activities at school: band, orchestra, or choir; school play or school musical; art club or art activities
CULTPOS	Cultural possessions index
female	female = 1; male = 0
HEDRES	Home educational resources index
LEADCOM	School leadership: Framing and communicating the school's goals and curricular development
	Frequency of the following statements:
	• I use student performance results to develop the school's educational goals
	• I make sure that the professional development activities of teachers are in accordance with the teaching goals of the school
	• I ensure that teachers work according to the school's educational goals
	• I discuss the school's academic goals with teachers at faculty meetings
LEADINST	School leadership: Instructional leadership
	• I promote teaching practices based on recent educational research
	• I praise teachers whose students are actively participating in learning
	• I draw teachers' attention to the importance of pupils' development of critical and social capacities
LEADPD	School leadership: Promoting instructional improvements and professional development
	• When a teacher has problems in his or her classroom, I take the initiative to discuss matters
	• I pay attention to disruptive behavior in classrooms
	• When a teacher brings up a classroom problem, we solve the problem together

table continues next page

Table 7A.1 Description of PISA Variables *(continued)*

Variable	Description
LEADTCH	School leadership: Teacher participation in leadership
	• I provide staff with opportunities to participate in school decision making
	• I engage teachers to help build a school culture of continuous improvement
	• I ask teachers to participate in reviewing management practices
mixed	Mixed secondary school = 1
PARED	Highest parental education in years
Ppressure	1 = face achievement pressure from many parents; 0 = pressure from minority of parents or absent
preschool	1 = attended preschool for at least a year
PROPQUAL	Proportion of teachers with tertiary qualification
public	Public school = 1
RESPCUR	Index of school responsibility for curriculum and assessment
	School principals' report regarding who had responsibility for four aspects of curriculum and assessment: "Establishing student assessment policies," "Choosing which textbooks are used," "Determining course content," and "Deciding which courses are offered." The index was calculated on the basis of the ratio of "yes" responses for school governing board, principal, or teachers on the one hand to "yes" responses for regional or local educational authority or national educational authority on the other hand.
RESPRES	Index of school responsibility for resource allocation
	School principals' report regarding who had considerable responsibility for tasks related to resource allocation ("Selecting teachers for hire," "Firing teachers," "Establishing teachers' starting salaries," "Determining teachers' salaries increases," "Formulating the school budget," "Deciding on budget allocations within the school"). The index was calculated on the basis of the ratio of "yes" responses for the school governing board, principal, or teachers to "yes" responses for regional or local educational authority or national educational authority.
SCMATBUI	Quality of physical infrastructure
	Is your school's capacity to provide instruction hindered by any of the following issues?
	• Shortage or inadequacy of school buildings and grounds
	• Shortage or inadequacy of heating/cooling and lighting systems
	• Shortage or inadequacy of instructional space (for example, classrooms)
SCMATEDU	Quality of school educational resources
	Is your school's capacity to provide instruction hindered by any of the following issues?
	• Shortage or inadequacy of science laboratory equipment
	• Shortage or inadequacy of instructional materials (for example, textbooks)
	• Shortage or inadequacy of computers for instruction
	• Lack or inadequacy of Internet connectivity
	• Shortage or inadequacy of computer software for instruction
	• Shortage or inadequacy of library materials
scoretrack	1 = achievement tracked by authority
Shortage_subject	1 = a lack of qualified [subject] teachers
STRATIO	Student-to-teacher ratio
STUDCLIM	Student-related factors affecting school climate
	In your school, to what extent is the learning of students hindered by the following phenomena?
	• Student truancy
	• Students skipping classes
	• Students arriving late for school
	• Students not attending compulsory school events

table continues next page

Table 7A.1 Description of PISA Variables *(continued)*

Variable	Description
	• Students lacking respect for teachers
	• Disruption of classes by students
	• Student use of alcohol or illegal drugs
	• Students intimidating or bullying other students
TCMORALE	Teacher morale
	Think about the teachers in your school. How much do you agree with the following statements?
	• The morale of teachers in this school is high
	• Teachers work with enthusiasm
	• Teachers take pride in this school
	• Teachers value academic achievement
TCSHORT	Index on teacher shortage
TEACCLIM	Teacher-related factors affecting school climate
	In your school, to what extent is the learning of students hindered by the following phenomena?
	• Students not being encouraged to achieve their full potential
	• Poor student-teacher relations
	• Teachers having to teach students of heterogeneous ability levels within the same class
	• Teachers having to teach students of diverse ethnic backgrounds (that is, language, culture) within the same class
	• Teachers' low expectations of students
	• Teachers not meeting individual students' needs
	• Teacher absenteeism
	• Staff resisting change
	• Teachers being too strict with students
	• Teachers being late for classes
	• Teachers not being well prepared for classes
WEALTH	Family wealth index

Source: OECD 2012, PISA 2012 database (http://pisa2012.acer.edu.au/).
Note: PISA = Programme for International Student Assessment.

Notes

1. PISA defines a public school as one managed directly or indirectly by a public education authority, government agency, or governing board appointed by government or elected by public franchise; and a private school as one managed directly or indirectly by a nongovernmental organization (for example, a church, trade union, business, or other private institution).

2. Similar and consistent results are found in the program-specific regression models using school characteristics, as presented in the previous section, indicating that the effects of individual and family characteristics are robust to the inclusion or exclusion of specific school characteristics and restriction of samples to a specific program.

3. Proportion of subcategory questions that students have successfully solved (that is, achieved full credit for).

References

OECD (Organisation for Economic Co-operation and Development). 2012. PISA 2012 (database). OECD, Paris, http://pisa2012.acer.edu.au/.

———. 2013. *PISA 2012 Assessment and Analytical Framework: Mathematics, Reading, Science, Problem Solving and Financial Literacy.* Paris: OECD Publishing. http://dx.doi.org/10.1787/9789264190511-en.

———. 2014. *PISA 2012 Results: Creative Problem Solving: Students' Skills in Tackling Real-Life Problems,* Volume V. Paris: OECD Publishing. http://dx.doi.org/10.1787/9789264208070-en.

Spiezia, Vincenzo. 2011. "Does Computer Use Increase Educational Achievements? Student-Level Evidence from PISA." *OECD Journal: Economic Studies* 7 (1): 1–22.

CHAPTER 8

Summary and Discussion

Introduction

This report documents and benchmarks key policies in basic education in Shanghai (see appendix A). It also provides evidence on the extent to which these policies have been implemented at the school level and throughout the system and, where possible, links implementation with learning outcomes as demonstrated in the Programme for International Student Assessment (PISA). The World Bank's Systems Approach for Better Education Results (SABER) benchmarking tools in various domains were used as the framework for collecting data and organizing the report. School-based surveys and other existing data and research were also tapped extensively to shed further light on implementation and on impact, if any. Finally, PISA 2012 data were explicitly used to analyze variations in student achievement within Shanghai and to examine which student, family, and school-level variables are correlated with the variation in student performance. The report was able, for the first time, to analyze policy factors that contribute to problem-solving skills beyond mathematical, reading, and scientific literacy.

What is particularly outstanding about Shanghai is that it has a very high degree of coherence between policy and implementation. Education policies are implemented very well in Shanghai. No large divergence between policy statements and reality on the ground is observed, as is constantly witnessed in other systems. This exceptional connection between policy and implementation can be attributed partly to the cultural and historical Chinese characteristics of top-down and centralized control by government authorities, and partly to high levels of professional accountability among various stakeholder groups within the education system. Close monitoring ensures that the programs and policies mandated by the government are executed smoothly with fairly high levels of compliance.

Shanghai further distinguishes itself by its constant drive to renew and improve. The policy stocktaking exercise permitted not just the current policies to be examined, but also the evolution of policies in many areas. Clearly Shanghai has been on a relentless crusade to update education policies in line with its social and economic development. Ever since China opened up to the world in the 1800s when western missionaries established new western-style schools, Shanghai has been on a journey of education reform. During the past three decades, and in particular since the end of the Cultural Revolution (1966–76), the Chinese government has called for rounds of education reform. Three typical strategic documents so far have guided the overall direction of reform: (1) the State Council's 1988 "Decisions about Education System Reform," (2) the State Council's 1999 "Decisions on Deepening Education Reform and Promoting Quality-Oriented Education in an All-Round Way," and (3) the State Council's 2010 "China's Medium- and Long-Term Education Reform and Development Plan Outline." Shanghai closely followed the course of the central government's reform course and has been pushing education reform accordingly.

The policy domains reviewed include teachers, school finance, school autonomy and accountability, and school assessment. The analysis concludes that based on SABER's framework and rubrics for scoring (with underlying benchmarks), Shanghai has achieved an overall score of "established" and "advanced" in almost every area except in two specific goals: "role of school council in governance" and "school accountability," both of which were rated as "emerging."

Clear expectations have been established for teachers and the teaching profession. Shanghai's education authorities have promulgated clear, documented guidelines for teachers to follow on grade-wise and subject-wise learning objectives, curriculum design, teaching-learning materials, and evaluation methods for all levels of schooling from first grade through twelfth grade. The Teachers Law of the People's Republic of China (1993) defines teachers' general obligations and working hours. In Shanghai, teachers' responsibilities go beyond the classroom to encompass extracurricular activities and professional development.

The system tends to attract the best candidates to enter the teaching profession. Teaching in Shanghai is a socially well regarded and monetarily appealing profession, with a proven set of entry requirements. The working conditions, such as infrastructure facilities and student-to-teacher ratio, are attractive, and clear career advancement mechanisms are in place. Most teaching candidates graduate from high-quality and systematic preservice teacher training programs. Additionally, an extensive in-service teacher training program is linked with career advancement and financial incentives. Professional development activities are designed to be collaborative and to pay particular attention to instructional improvement. School leaders are responsible for creating targeted teacher training plans based on evaluation results for each teacher. Weak and inexperienced teachers are paired with high-performing and experienced ones. Teaching-research groups and lesson observations are two common and successful practices. A set of incentive policies is in place to reward teachers' achievements and best practices.

Clear standards for selection and performance of school principals are in place and principals are expected to be instructional leaders. Requirements for principals are stringent across Shanghai, although they vary from one district to another. Supported by various leadership training programs, school principals in

Shanghai appear to play an extensive role in managing schools. They benefit from various monetary and nonmonetary performance-based incentives, and they play an influential role in curricular reforms and instructional development. An effective practice is in place of principal-led monitoring and evaluation of classroom instruction; constant evaluation of the efficacy of the curriculum; and communication with students, teachers, and parents. Principals exercise significant autonomy over various school-level decisions such as hiring of teachers and determining the performance-based portions of their salaries. Multiple systems are in place that monitor and evaluate teacher performance, promote research activities led by teachers, and encourage collaborative processes among teaching staff.

Shanghai's public expenditure on education as a share of GDP was about 3.5 percent in 2013, relatively small compared with other high-performing economies such as Finland, Japan, the Republic of Korea, and the United States. However, education financing in Shanghai is structured not only to provide minimum inputs and ensure minimum outputs, but also to lift the learning outcomes of all students by specifically targeting low-performing schools and districts. Shanghai has discarded the rather inequitable "key school" system in basic education. Innovative financing instruments such as "entrusted management," which twins a low-performing school with a high-performing peer through a memorandum of understanding backed by government financing, is rapidly gaining support. This approach stands in stark contrast to practices in other countries that reward top-performing schools and hope to "weed out" low-performing schools.

The analysis finds that clear and detailed policy tools are in place to ensure basic educational inputs in safe and adequate infrastructure, teaching-learning materials, professional development avenues, and appropriate class-size norms. Shanghai's education system has established learning goals with regard to completion, progression, and knowledge and skills.

An extensive system of student evaluations at various grade levels allows education authorities to relate outcomes to educational inputs, thereby allowing them to provide extra support to low-performing areas in the form of topical teacher training, additional management support from better-performing schools, and other relevant resources. Specific authorities are delegated the responsibility to monitor service delivery, such as establishing annual academic calendars, ensuring timely delivery of books for students and teaching aids for teachers, overseeing necessary construction activities within school premises, checking teacher attendance, substituting for occasional teacher absences, and more. A regimented, well-informed, and fairly transparent process for budgetary allocations affords schools sufficient autonomy to express their needs.

Shanghai is a trendsetter in its execution of specific policies to support disadvantaged individuals, communities, schools, and districts. With specific support programs and policies for children from low-income families and from migrant families, Shanghai has made relatively more progress in attaining equal and equitable access to schooling than any other region of the country. By eliminating the selective and elite key school system at the basic education level and promoting "entrusted management" of schools, Shanghai has contributed immensely to the national education policies directed toward capacity building of weak schools. However, greater attention is required to strengthen the implementation of special education policies. A closely monitored and managed system for verifying expenses on educational resources through well-instituted system-wide processes for auditing has enabled Shanghai to achieve "advanced" ratings on efficient management of resources.

An investigation of the various policy provisions and outcomes related to autonomy and accountability found that the school budget planning and management processes are fairly participatory, with schools taking the initiative in preparing their operational budgets. Decisions regarding salary structures for teaching and nonteaching staff are relatively centralized and carried out in a top-down manner. Nevertheless, district-level authorities have some discretion in creating specific salary disbursement standards for teaching and nonteaching staff. Overall, it was observed that Shanghai's private school principals tend to exercise greater autonomy over staff and remuneration-related decisions than do public school principals. This variation is consistent with the school council management structure required for private schools and lack of the same for public schools. Establishment of parent-teacher associations is a fairly new concept in the region and has yet to effectively engage parents and the wider community in various processes of school management. Currently, at the school level, principals have the greatest autonomy over day-to-day teaching, learning, management, and reform initiatives.

Schools are explicitly required to conform to financial management guidelines and other broad city-level requirements. Additionally, schools receive an annual supervisory visit and are further subject to the comprehensive school evaluation using the "Green Indicators of Academic Quality of Primary and Secondary School Students." However, Shanghai has made a deliberate effort to not use student exam results as an explicit mechanism for rewards or sanctions. In reality, of course, the high-stakes exams at the end of lower secondary and upper secondary school tend to influence the learning priorities in lower grades, and overall, schools continue to be assessed on the basis of their performance on these tests.

Professional accountability is maintained through inherent relations within the teaching staff and through the execution of in-service teacher training and monitoring procedures. School principals and senior teachers engage with others through elaborate teaching-research groups and constantly monitor and support them to improve their instruction and knowledge, so professional accountability becomes more apparent and more positively related with competence.

The common formats for student assessment used in China and Shanghai are continuous and formative classroom assessments; summative examinations, particularly at the end of ninth and twelfth grades; and national and international large-scale assessments. Classroom assessments are frequent and are executed in a variety of formats, such as quizzes, oral tests, presentations, home assignments, and so forth. This form of assessment allows students a wider variety of ways to demonstrate their learning than afforded by summative examinations in the form of written tests. Clear guidelines have been established for assessment standards, and efforts have been made to align these standards with appropriately age-relevant expected learning outcomes. Additionally, efforts are made to monitor the quality of assessments at the school level, and the data are effectively used to inform teaching-learning and future assessment practices in the classroom. To improve classroom assessment, the municipal and district-level Teaching Research Offices undertake regular research projects on the status of student assessments to inform policy decisions. Examinations are summative, formal procedures that are mostly used for the purpose of making decisions regarding a student's advancement to the successive level of schooling.

Senior secondary school entrance exams and senior secondary graduation exams are conducted for all graduates every year. These exams, primarily for selection purposes, are well-recognized social events in Shanghai and are closely followed by students, parents, educators, and the media. A well-structured system is in place with clear policy guidelines, regular funding, and sufficient and well-trained human resources to enable effective execution of these exams. These exams are aligned with the learning goals for students and teachers. The exams are considered of good quality and the process overall is transparent and fair. However, these are primarily selection exams and are being blamed for putting tremendous pressure on students and motivating schools and teachers to teach to the tests.

Shanghai is one of the pioneer Chinese cities to have participated in large-scale international assessments. The city's students performed exceptionally well on the 2009 and 2012 PISA and garnered significant national and international attention for their educational success. The enabling context for Shanghai's participation in PISA, which includes the presence of clear policy guidelines, necessary funding, and effective human resources, was assessed at the "advanced" level. However, the city's education system scored rather poorly on its policy goal of ensuring effective use of the data generated through such international assessments. This finding reiterates the earlier observation in chapter 5 that Shanghai's attention to a post-evaluation plan of action is disproportionately low.

The report also examines the extent to which Shanghai's education policies and practices foster learning outcomes, as revealed in the 2012 PISA results. In 2012, Shanghai continued to be the top performer on all three major domains of PISA (mathematics, reading, and science). Additionally, Shanghai emerged as one of the most equal education systems among PISA participants, with the highest proportion of disadvantaged students performing among the top 25 percent of students across all participating countries and economies after controlling for socioeconomic status. In a comparison of the performance of students in Shanghai, significant variation was found across programs, with upper secondary students performing better than lower secondary, and model or experimental senior secondary school students performing better than those from vocational schools. Overall, model or experimental upper secondary school students scored the highest across all three domains—mathematics, science, and reading.

How Shanghai Does It • http://dx.doi.org/10.1596/978-1-4648-0790-9

The learning outcome disparity by program is in part due to the system's tracking of students at the end of lower secondary schooling. However, the analysis was also able to show that within each program type, policies and practices at the school level still play a significant role in explaining students' PISA performance. The findings confirm much of the existing education policy research for across the globe.

Factors Associated with Mathematical, Reading, and Scientific Literacy

Among junior secondary students, students in schools that offered more creative extracurricular activities performed better across mathematics, reading, and science. Private junior secondary school students (accounting for 10 percent of the total lower secondary student population) performed significantly better than public school students on mathematics and reading. Moreover, junior secondary schools with more autonomy in determining curriculum and assessment actually experienced lower performance on mathematics.

Among upper secondary students, teacher participation in school leadership is significantly related to higher mathematics and reading scores. Quality of school educational resources is also positively related to reading performance. The 2009 PISA data also show a higher level of teacher participation in school governance and better educational resources among better-performing schools.

Among vocational students, schools with better mathematics performance tend to have fewer student-related factors affecting school climate, consistent with what was found in the 2009 PISA assessment. Schools facing pressure from parents have higher mean mathematics scores than those who do not. The scientific literacy of vocational school students is positively and significantly related to schools' quality of physical infrastructure, class sizes, and availability of creative extracurricular activities.

In addition, individual and family background characteristics demonstrate a consistent relationship with student performance across academic programs. Girls perform significantly worse on mathematics and science, and better on reading, than boys, consistent with findings from other PISA participants (OECD 2015). Home educational resources, cultural possessions, and parental education levels exhibit a positive relationship with student reading literacy. In contrast, family wealth is negatively related to performance. Finally, students who have attended at least a year of preschool perform significantly better on all three domains.

Factors Associated with Problem-Solving Skills

Similar to mathematics, reading, and science, better problem-solving skills are exhibited among general upper secondary students compared with lower secondary students and vocational students. Model or experimental senior secondary school students demonstrate higher problem-solving skills than ordinary senior secondary school students.

For lower secondary students, problem-solving skills are significantly and positively related to quality of school educational resources and principals' instructional leadership, after controlling for mathematics, reading, and science performance. For general upper secondary students, schools with higher student-to-teacher ratios and those that face competition from other schools tend to have students who perform better on problem solving, although the relationship seems to be accounted for by differences in performance on mathematics, reading, and science.

Among vocational students, problem-solving skills are related to a number of school characteristics. Holding mathematics, science, and reading performance constant, vocational schools with smaller student-to-teacher ratios and class sizes have better problem-solving scores. Vocational schools with more autonomy over curriculum and assessment policies and whose academic performance is not tracked by any education authority perform better on problem solving, and the difference remains even after controlling for mathematical, reading, and scientific literacy. Among various dimensions of school leadership, schools with better problem-solving performance have principals who more often promote institutional improvements and professional development, but less often demonstrate instructional leadership. There is a significant advantage in problem-solving skills among private vocational school students over public ones, but the gap seems to be accounted for by performance on mathematics, reading, and science. Similarly, vocational schools faced with parental pressure score higher on problem solving, but the difference disappears once mathematical, reading, and scientific literacy are accounted for.

Among individual characteristics, girls have lower problem-solving skills than boys, regardless of specific nature or process (see chapter 7 for discussions of problem-solving nature and process), and the disadvantage seems to be independent of their disadvantage in mathematics and science, as observed before. Holding mathematical, reading, and scientific literacy constant, family wealth is significantly correlated with students' higher problem-solving skills, while family cultural possessions are negatively related to problem-solving scores. The positive relationship between home educational resources and problem-solving skills seems to be partially accounted for by variations in mathematical, reading, and scientific literacy.

Several family background characteristics are also associated with student skills in solving problems of a specific nature. For example, family cultural possessions are associated with higher odds of solving static problems, while home educational resources are associated with higher odds of solving interactive problems. Parental education level is associated with higher probability of solving problems involving "representing and formulating" processes.

Students who have attended at least a year of preschool have better problem-solving scores, but the advantage seems to be accounted for by mathematical, reading, and scientific literacy. Preschool attendance is also related to higher odds of solving interactive problems, and problems involving "planning and execution" and "monitoring and reflecting processes."

How Shanghai Does It • http://dx.doi.org/10.1596/978-1-4648-0790-9

Policy Considerations for Shanghai

PISA and SABER do not entirely capture the intricacies of Shanghai's education system and the aspirations that have evolved through a rich history of local reforms. Shanghai has moved far beyond the PISA and is formulating and projecting new goals and visions. Nevertheless, the comprehensive assessment of Shanghai's education policies provides an opportunity to reflect on a few policy considerations. The following list of policy considerations was arrived at after a series of consultations carried out with education thinkers and authorities in Shanghai during the process of this study. Further interactions were carried out during the drafting of the "Shanghai Education: Vision 2050" document by the World Bank through a comprehensive review of global policy literature and interactions with education policy makers in Shanghai. These considerations are intended to facilitate further discussions in Shanghai as well as in other aspiring education systems.

Consider delaying tracking to tenth grade or later. Evidence from Poland and Germany shows that delaying tracking and extending students' time with general academic education to develop basic competencies in reading and mathematics could increase overall academic performance (Jakubowski and others 2016; Muhlenweg 2007). The *zhong kao* exam after ninth grade tracks students into three distinct senior secondary school programs with very little horizontal mobility between them. Cumulative differences in endowment in teachers and other resources further accentuate the disparity in education quality among the programs. Shanghai could potentially pilot eliminating the *zhong kao* and delaying tracking to tenth or twelfth grades like other advanced nations and providing more curriculum diversification.

Increase assistance to migrant and other disadvantaged children. Shanghai proactively enacted policies and approaches to expanding education services to migrant and other disadvantaged children. But the current eligibility criteria of three years of residency and employment may need to be relaxed to allow more migrant children to enroll in local public or government-sponsored private schools. "Disadvantaged" children are required to update their status every year to qualify for assistance, which could ostracize them further. The city does not allow migrant children to enroll in its public senior secondary schools, limiting their potential.

Expand the role of parents, the community, and society in education. Parent-teacher associations are a fairly new concept and tend to have limited responsibilities. At the same time, many anecdotes and isolated studies seem to indicate that there is some dissatisfaction with the public education system. Shanghai could consider expanding the role of parents, the community, and society in general in the education system.

Formally upgrade teacher entry qualifications to make the profession even more attractive. Require at least a bachelor's degree as a teacher entry criterion. Doing so will place Shanghai on par with most Organisation for Economic Co-operation and Development countries and other developed Asian countries. Most applicants already have bachelor's degrees, so the higher requirement will reduce unnecessary recruitment inefficiency.

Further reduce the allocation disparity of talented teachers and other resources among schools. Highly qualified teachers should be more evenly dispersed between rural and urban districts and between model schools and regular schools. SABER does not fully address this issue, and researchers should analyze the matter further. Qualified special education teachers may also be unevenly distributed. And as Shanghai includes more special education students in regular classrooms, demand for special education–trained teachers will increase.

Invest more in information and communications technology. Although 95 percent of schools indicate that their student registration profiles are completely or mostly in an electronic format, only 72 percent have student growth profiles (with more detailed student achievement information) and 67 percent have teacher professional development profiles completely or mostly in an electronic format. Shanghai should invest more in technology.

Further explore the role of public-private partnerships to address the last-mile issues in education service delivery. Promising initiatives such as entrusted management of low-performing schools and purchase of education services from private providers could be scaled up and formally institutionalized.

In the past few decades, Shanghai has grown rapidly into a global economic and commercial capital. As assessments such as PISA have shown, it is also leading the world in basic education. This includes many educational areas—from attracting and developing high-caliber teachers to using financial and other resources to ensure that every child, regardless of background, has access to a top-flight education. The city wants to continue to forge ahead with education reform, closing the quality and accessibility gap even more. As the Shanghai education system continues to achieve a high level of basic cognitive achievement, there will be renewed discussion on how the current curriculum and pedagogy promote students' social and emotional well-being and twenty-first century skills such as global citizenship and environmental consciousness.

It will be increasingly important for Shanghai to find a healthier balance between academic excellence and students' social and emotional well-being. Though not explicitly discussed in this report, students in Shanghai report a high level of parental pressure and unhappiness when compared with their international peers. Society and government need to find a balance between academic excellence and the social and emotional well-being of the younger generation.

Pressure will also intensify to further expand early childhood education, delay tracking at the secondary level, and improve the relevance of higher education and training levels. Shanghai could further encourage institutions to engage in evidence-based education research and public education debates. It could also continue to build a virtuous cycle of reform and development toward an education system that is even more competitive globally.

References

Jakubowski, M., H. A. Patrinos, E. E. Porta, and J. Wiśniewski. 2016. "The Effects of Delaying Tracking in Secondary School: Evidence from the 1999 Education Reform in Poland." *Education Economics*. doi: 10.1080/09645292.2016.1149548.

Muhlenweg, A. 2007. "Educational Effects of Early or Later Secondary School Tracking in Germany." Centre for European Economic Research. ftp://ftp.zew.de/pub/zew-docs /dp/dp07079.pdf.

OECD (Organisation for Economic Co-operation and Development). 2015. *The ABC of Gender Equality in Education: Aptitude, Behaviour, Confidence*. Paris: OECD Publishing. http://dx.doi.org/10.1787/9789264229945-en.

Summary of Shanghai's Basic Education Policy Environment by the World Bank–SABER Policy Framework

Table A.1 Shanghai's Status under SABER Policy Goals

Policy domain	Policy goals	Status
Attracting and Developing an Excellent Teaching Force	**1. Setting clear expectation for teachers** Clear policies are in place to provide overall guidelines on learning objectives, curriculum structure and design, teaching-learning materials, and an evaluation system for all subjects across all grade levels. Additionally, the Teachers Law of the PRC (1993) defines the general obligations of teachers and their working hours. In Shanghai, teacher responsibilities go beyond the classroom to encompass extracurricular activities and professional development.	Advanced ●●●●
	2. Attracting the best into teaching Teaching in Shanghai is a socially well regarded and monetarily appealing profession, with a proven set of entry requirements. The working conditions, such as infrastructure facilities and student-to-teacher ratio, are attractive, and clear career advancement mechanisms are in place.	Advanced ●●●●
	3. Preparing teachers with useful training and experience Shanghai requires a minimum three-year vocational tertiary education for primary school teachers and a four-year university education for secondary school teachers. In practice, however, the academic requirement is more stringent. Of the schools surveyed, 97 percent have a minimum academic requirement of a four-year bachelor's degree when making hiring decisions. The initial teacher education programs in China tend to provide high-quality subject content knowledge and require an average six-month practicum. The policy requirement for preservice teacher qualification could be enhanced to reflect actual practice (a minimum of a four-year university degree) to reduce unnecessary inefficiency in the recruiting process and to send a positive signal for the teaching profession.	Established ●●●○

table continues next page

Table A.1 Shanghai's Status under SABER Policy Goals (continued)

Policy domain	Policy goals	Status
	4. Matching teachers' skills with students' needs Numerous incentives are offered to teachers to teach in hard-to-staff rural and semi-urban schools. Temporary transfers and rotations are made to help underperforming schools and disadvantaged student populations. Shanghai is not faced with critical shortages of teachers in any particular subjects. However, further research would be helpful to gather a clearer picture of demand and supply features of teachers' skills and students' needs.	Established ●●●○
	5. Leading teachers with strong principals Recruitment criteria for school principals are high and practiced stringently. However, the qualifications vary across districts. Principals in Shanghai participate in various leadership programs, based on the "Professional Standards for Basic Education Principals," over the course of their tenure. Part of their remuneration is linked to the overall performance of their schools. Principals play an instrumental role in designing instruction and monitoring and evaluating teaching activities within their schools. They have substantial autonomy in decisions related to pedagogic practices and teacher management, such as hiring and rewarding teachers.	Established ●●●○
	6. Monitoring teaching and learning Adequate data on student learning outcomes are available to inform teaching and policy. Results from a series of formative and summative student assessments serve a diagnostic purpose, encouraging teachers to identify areas of improvement in instructional practice, as well as helping schools analyze their teachers' existing strengths and weaknesses to tailor professional development opportunities. Based on the State Council's 2012 "Advice on Strengthening the Teaching Force," teacher performance is monitored comprehensively through multiple mechanisms, and not solely on the basis of students' academic performance. Frequent district-level inspections of teachers' work and classroom observations by senior teachers and principals are some of the common monitoring and evaluation processes.	Advanced ●●●●
	7. Supporting teachers to improve instruction New teachers are required to complete at least 360 hours of professional development within the first five years of service, and an additional 540 hours to be considered for a senior rank. Professional development is a substantial part of schools' operational expenditures. Professional development activities are designed to be collaborative and to pay particular attention to instructional improvement. School leaders are responsible for creating targeted teacher training plans based on the evaluation results for each teacher. Weak and inexperienced teachers are paired with high-performing and experienced ones. Teaching-research groups and lesson observations are two common and successful practices. However, compared with other countries (Japan, the Republic of Korea, and Singapore) the required number of professional development hours in Shanghai is low.	Established ●●●○
	8. Motivating teachers to perform better Promotion opportunities are linked to performance. The "Guidelines for Regular Accreditation of Primary and Secondary Teachers" require teachers to be accredited once every five years to continue teaching. According to the Teachers Law of the PRC, teachers can be dismissed for misconduct, child abuse, and poor performance. A small proportion of teacher pay is also linked to workload and performance. Further research is required on the relationship between the teaching career ladder and the performance pay system in Shanghai.	Established ●●●○

table continues next page

Table A.1 Shanghai's Status under SABER Policy Goals (continued)

Policy domain	Policy goals	Status
Financing Education for Quality and Equity	**1. Ensuring basic conditions for learning** Detailed policies and regulations are in place to ensure basic educational inputs of infrastructure, learning materials, teacher qualifications, and staffing norms. However, in practice, disparities are evident across public and private, and city and rural schools. With regard to completion, progression, and knowledge and skills, the city has a well-established set of learning goals for basic education.	Advanced ●●●●
	2. Monitoring and evaluating learning conditions and outcomes Both the school environment and teaching-learning outcomes are closely monitored. School- and district-level data are collected and compiled by the municipality annually. However, Shanghai needs to improve its use of information technology in collecting school data. The "Green Indicators of Academic Quality of Primary and Secondary School Students," in place since 2011, annually assess school quality holistically, including learning motivation, academic burden, and student-teacher relationships.	Established ●●●○
	3. Overseeing service delivery Shanghai has established a city-level system to track effective school days and mechanisms to monitor the availability of learning materials and physical resources at schools. Shanghai has an established mechanism to verify teacher attendance as well as the need for substitute teachers in case of absences.	Established ●●●○
	4. Budgeting with adequate and transparent information The "Provision on Budget Management for Institutions" under Shanghai Municipal Education Commission specifies the criteria for education funding. Education budgeting is underpinned by adequate and transparent information that is made available to the public. Mechanisms are in place to collect data at the school and district levels to support future budget planning with specific requirements.	Established ●●●○
	5. Providing more resources to students in need Shanghai has specific policies to assist students from disadvantaged backgrounds with education expenses, such as free school meals for migrant children and students from families below the poverty line, and education subsidies to students with disabilities or economic hardships. However, "disadvantaged" students are required to update their status every year. Underperforming schools are being supported through innovative programs such as "entrusted management." Greater efforts need to be made to improve opportunities for migrant children and students with disabilities.	Established ●●●○
	6. Managing resources efficiently Systems are in place to verify the use of educational resources, but coverage can be expanded. Under the "Regulations on Primary and Secondary School Finance," schools in Shanghai have to use allocated funding within the defined categories and submit detailed expenditure reports. Internal (school-level) and external (Municipal and District Audit Offices) audits are carried out to verify the use of resources. Schools that fail internal or external audits receive legal sanctions.	Advanced ●●●●
Balancing Autonomy and Accountability	**1. Level of autonomy in planning and management of the school budget** Budget planning is a collaborative and multistep process involving schools. After receiving the budget approved by the district Department of Finance and the municipal government, schools have the autonomy to execute the budget under defined categories. Schools have limited influence on teachers' base pay scale, which is set at the municipal level, but they do have autonomy in determining the allocation of performance pay. Schools tend to have relatively more say in determining the salaries of nonteaching staff. Compared with private schools, public schools tend to have less autonomy, particularly in their ability to raise funds.	Established ●●●○

table continues next page

Table A.1 Shanghai's Status under SABER Policy Goals *(continued)*

Policy domain	Policy goals	Status
	2. Level of autonomy in personnel management Districts in Shanghai vary in the degree of school-level autonomy for appointing and dismissing teachers. The authority to hire is significantly greater than the authority to dismiss. The hiring and deployment process for nonteaching staff is relatively more flexible. Shanghai has no uniform municipal-level policy on the appointment and deployment of principals, but districts have the authority to establish their own processes.	Established ●●●○
	3. Role of the school council in school governance Public schools are not mandated to have school councils but follow the "school principal responsibility system," whereby principals make key decisions, usually in consultation with the party secretaries and increasingly in consultation with the teacher staff association. Private schools in Shanghai, by law, are required to establish "school boards" that have wider representation. Although the board participates in decision making about general planning and budgeting, it is generally not involved in professional matters concerning teaching and learning. Parent-teacher associations have existed since 2012, but their role is confined to supporting basic school management tasks and home education of children. There is no city-level policy, guideline, or manual regulating the participation of the community or the school council in school activities and learning inputs.	Emerging ●●○○
	4. School and student assessment A well-established and frequently administered system of formative and summative assessments in schools is used to regularly inform teaching practices and make necessary adjustments. Citywide and nationwide standardized assessments are conducted annually, most prominently at the end of ninth grade and twelfth grade. The data from these assessments help policy makers track trends in student learning outcomes.	Established ●●●○
	5. School accountability Clear city- and district-level guidelines govern the use of results from student assessments. However, the data, details of which are often not made public, could be more effectively analyzed. Schools in Shanghai have to strictly comply with the national "Elementary and Secondary School Finance Policy," which lays out detailed rules for the management of budget, revenue, expenditure, surplus, and capital assets. Failure to comply leads to legal sanctions. Policy guidelines are in place for regulating financial management and transparency standards in private schools. However, there are no explicit policies and mechanisms for learning accountability toward stakeholders in the form of public forums. Communities and parents tend to explicitly entrust education professionals with the management of professional affairs and education institutions.	Emerging ●●○○
Creating an Effective Student Assessment System	**1. Classroom assessment (Enabling context, System alignment, and Assessment quality)** In 2013 the Shanghai Municipal Education Commission released "Advice on Curriculum-Standards-Based Teaching and Assessments at the Primary School Level" to instruct teachers on carrying out teaching activities and assessments in accordance with the curriculum standards. Classroom assessment is a core aspect of a teacher's professional development and performance evaluation.	Established ●●●○
	2. Examinations—lower secondary graduation (Enabling context, System alignment, and Assessment quality) The *zhong kao* exams at the end of ninth grade provide the selection criterion for high school entrance, and are indicative of the overall status of the basic education system. Formal policy documents authorize and guide the processes of this exam, and the municipal government allocates regular funding and the	Established ●●●○

table continues next page

Table A.1 **Shanghai's Status under SABER Policy Goals** *(continued)*

Policy domain	Policy goals	Status
	necessary human resources. Based on the 2009 "Advice on Designing Lower Secondary School Graduation Examination in Shanghai," a systematic method is used to select and organize teachers for the design and scoring of *zhong kao*, as well as to maintain standards of quality and fairness.	
	3. Examinations—senior secondary graduation (Enabling context, System alignment, and Assessment quality) *Gao kao* is a high-stakes competitive exam that determines college entrance for twelfth grade graduates. The exam is based on the national curriculum guidelines and standards. The National Examination Center takes the lead in designing the national *gao kao*, and province-specific *gao kao* questions are developed by provincial-level *gao kao* committees. Funding for *gao kao* preparation and implementation is a regular component of local education expenditures under the 2014 "Regulations on Tertiary Institutions Admission." The *gao kao* undergoes a rigorous quality assurance procedure, including internal and external review, external certification, pilot, and translation verification. The passing rates of the exam are closely monitored by oversight committees and expert review groups.	Advanced
	4. National large-scale assessment (Enabling context, System alignment, and Assessment quality) The State Council formally rolled out the Plan for National Compulsory Education Quality Monitoring in April 2015. The plan outlines an annual sample-based assessment in two different subject areas for fourth- and eighth-grade students, and covers six main subject areas (Chinese, mathematics, science, physical education, art, and moral education) over a three-year period. The assessment was first administered on a nationwide basis in 2015. In addition, children in Shanghai are annually assessed on a relatively more holistic set of indicators ("Green Indicators of Academic Quality of Primary and Secondary School Students") launched by the Shanghai Educational Commission in 2011. To alleviate the fear that parents and children have of *gao kao* and *zhong kao*, Shanghai is currently piloting reforms to both tests and will roll out a revised and more flexible format in 2017–18.	Established
	5. International assessment (Enabling context, System alignment, and Assessment quality) In both 2009 and 2012, the city participated in the Programme for International Student Assessment (PISA). Although the performance of students in Shanghai on PISA has been outstanding as a result of its cutting-edge provisions for ensuring an enabling environment for conducting international evaluation, the city's performance with regard to professional development of teachers and postevaluation use of the PISA assessment data is rated "established," not "advanced."	Established ●●●○

Note: PRC = People's Republic of China; SABER = Systems Approach for Better Educational Results.

Environmental Benefits Statement

The World Bank Group is committed to reducing its environmental footprint. In support of this commitment, the Publishing and Knowledge Division leverages electronic publishing options and print-on-demand technology, which is located in regional hubs worldwide. Together, these initiatives enable print runs to be lowered and shipping distances decreased, resulting in reduced paper consumption, chemical use, greenhouse gas emissions, and waste.

The Publishing and Knowledge Division follows the recommended standards for paper use set by the Green Press Initiative. The majority of our books are printed on Forest Stewardship Council (FSC)–certified paper, with nearly all containing 50–100 percent recycled content. The recycled fiber in our book paper is either unbleached or bleached using totally chlorine-free (TCF), processed chlorine-free (PCF), or enhanced elemental chlorine-free (EECF) processes.

More information about the Bank's environmental philosophy can be found at http://www.worldbank.org/corporateresponsibility.